Ten Steps to ITSM Success

A Practitioner's Guide to Enterprise IT Transformation

Ten Steps to ITSM Success

A Practitioner's Guide to Enterprise IT Transformation

ANGELO ESPOSITO

TIMOTHY ROGERS

IT Governance Publishing

Every possible effort has been made to ensure that the information contained in this book is accurate at the time of going to press, and the publisher and the author cannot accept responsibility for any errors or omissions, however caused. Any opinions expressed in this book are those of the author, not the publisher. Websites identified are for reference only, not endorsement, and any website visits are always at the reader's own risk. No responsibility for loss or damage occasioned to any person acting, or refraining from action, as a result of the material in this publication can be accepted by the publisher or the author.

ITIL® is a registered trademark of the Cabinet Office.
COBIT 5® is a registered trademark of the ISACA®.

IT Governance Publishing
IT Governance Limited
Unit 3, Clive Court
Bartholomew's Walk
Cambridgeshire Business Park
Ely
Cambridgeshire
CB7 4EA
United Kingdom

www.itgovernance.co.uk

First published in the United Kingdom in 2013
by IT Governance Publishing.

ISBN 978-1-84928-456-1

FOREWORD

Every Service Management "adapt and adopt" initiative teaches some very hard lessons. Those who have read the books (or passed an ITIL® Foundation course) and think, "Ah! This will be easy!" soon learn the books are references and the need to read the "whitespace" is imperative. The "how to" is often hidden in the guidance, if only due to the endless variables any organization's culture presents. Finding a Service Manager with quality experience gained from success **and** failure is invaluable to any service improvement initiative. With today's limited or reducing budgets and an economy that demands fiscal responsibility, there is very little room for "learn as you go" approaches, or support for contagious enthusiasm without beneficial results and business value.

This is where Esposito and Rogers step in. In *Ten Steps to ITSM Success*, those hard-learned lessons are documented and explained in a manner that requires no "whitespace" reading and supposition. They provide a structure that is proven – its activities easy to understand and apply, no matter the environment. These activities are crucial to a successful Service Management initiative or, for that matter, any improvement activity. This information has been developed over a number of years of Service Management experience, as well as continuous refinement based on highly successful workshops. This book represents that core knowledge, as well as key supporting templates.

This is the guide that will assist the newly initiated Service Manager, as well as provide practical advice, guidance or justification for the experienced Service Manager. In any case, this is a book that has been needed for a long time in the Service Management community – a no-nonsense guide to deploying service-oriented functionality. Hats off to Esposito and Rogers for finally fulfilling that need!

This book represents the second volume in the itSMF USA *Thought Leadership* series. It has been an extreme honor to work with the many talents found within the membership of itSMF USA, and to produce the first two volumes. It has been an even higher honor working with Angelo and Tim in editing and reviewing this book. Congratulations, gentlemen, on a job well done!

Suzanne D. Van Hove, Ed.D., FSM®
CEO, SED-IT

Enterprise IT Transformation is a subject best understood by those who have felt the frustration and pain of having to deal with an ineffective and expensive IT infrastructure. It has been my experience that many IT professionals lose sight of their objectives because they feel constrained by defined limitations and current shortcomings. They use these constraints as excuses for delivering poor service. End-users accept poor service and ineffective IT because that's all they have. These accepted limitations "legitimize" ineffective IT.

The fundamental benefit of having, using and validating excuses is that most excuses are reasonable and defined. They articulate why things aren't one's fault. Good excuses are the mother's milk of the status quo.

If this is the case, then why would a person – end-user or IT professional – read this book? The answer to this question is quite simple: this book does not redefine, try to refocus or rebut excuses. It embraces change on its own terms and allows for genuine transformation based on identified needs, including the reality of accomplishing this in a real-world business environment. I personally know both authors and have used their counsel and advice. What they outline here works.

I was a military staff officer working on a United States Navy program responsible for the transformation of the Navy's enterprise network. This network is the largest IT network in the world, with complex and critical service requirements that support more than half a billion users. When first assigned, I knew political infighting and contractual considerations would complicate and impact the transformation effort. What I did not understand was there were some elements so disconnected from established and written requirements that accounting for, and including, them in the enterprise would represent significant challenges.

Desperate for a way to rein in cost, I identified and quantified key enterprise service requirements. Using an approach very similar to the one defined in this book, Angelo and Tim lead the effort to implement a practical approach consistent with Information Technology Infrastructure Library® (ITIL®) guidelines. This book does not rewrite ITIL®, or redefine Information Technology Service Management (ITSM); it articulates intent. It defines tools for the IT professional to use that promote effective process development, establish governance bodies and define key infrastructure elements. My best advice to both the IT professional and enterprise end-user: read this book.

Eugene Smith
Commander, USNR

PREFACE

ITIL®, COBIT®, ISO/IEC 20000 – which methodology should I choose? How do tools like Lean Six Sigma, CMMI® and the Balanced Scorecard® fit in? How do I leverage governance and project management principles to help transform the practice of IT Service Management (ITSM) in my organization?

Questions like these – and countless more just like them – prompted the creation of this book. We – and we are active practitioners and consultants, just like many of you – once asked the same set of questions. Faced with clients seeking to "adopt a Service Management culture," we were sometimes ordered to use the ITIL® framework exactly as presented in the library. Other clients preferred COBIT®. One client insisted on the Microsoft© Operations Framework (MOF©).

Based on our experience working with a number of organizations across industries, we firmly believe there is no single approach or framework that is perfectly suited to every organization. Rather, each organization is best served by adapting elements from the various frameworks, and using them in tandem – playing to each one's strengths – to achieve the desired results.

As organizations seek to increase revenue, expand markets, cut costs and increase efficiency, they increasingly look to IT as a strategic partner in achieving these objectives. This book helps IT prepare for this role by providing a very detailed, practical, hands-on guide to implementing ITSM best practices within an organization. Because of its agnostic approach, it can be used by any industry – regardless of size – around the world. Specific guidance is provided on forging agreement on enterprise ITSM strategy, establishing cross-organizational ITSM governance, managing organizational change, and developing enterprise ITSM process and continual improvement standards.

Although we use material from other frameworks in this Ten-Step approach, the primary focus remains the IT Infrastructure Library® (ITIL®). ITIL® is architected as a "complementary framework," and was never intended to stand alone. However, in our humble opinion, ITIL® is – and will continue to be for some time – the predominant and *de facto* standard for IT shops worldwide.

That being said, we also acknowledge that, no matter how good you are, there is always room for improvement – which is why we have produced this practical guide to achieving ITSM success. We believe we have discovered a rational, repeatable, flexible and customizable approach to the practice of IT Service Management. We hope that you will agree.

ABOUT THE AUTHORS

Angelo Esposito, Program Manager with Jacobs Technology, is currently advising the US Navy on its Enterprise ITSM Transformation effort. A former Chief Information Officer (CIO) with more than 25 years of experience, he has worked in commercial, non-profit and government sectors. Mr Esposito holds a degree from the University of Massachusetts, Boston, and certifications in ITIL®, Information Systems Auditing, Information Security Management, and the Governance of Enterprise IT.

In addition to the United States, Mr Esposito has lived and worked in England, Luxembourg and Canada. His hobbies include competing as a triathlete and participating as a Century bike rider for charitable causes. Mr Esposito currently resides in Washington, DC, USA.

Timothy Rogers is a consultant specializing in Enterprise Service Management, Transformation, Governance and Continual Improvement. A former Chief Technology Officer (CTO) with more than 15 years of experience, he has worked with high-tech startups, financial services firms, and large government clients, including the US Navy. Mr Rogers holds a Master's Degree from the University of California, San Diego, and certifications in ITIL®, ISO and Lean Six Sigma.

In addition to the United States, Mr Rogers has lived and worked in Hong Kong, and speaks some Mandarin Chinese. He serves on the Board of the itSMF USA San Diego Interest Group, is a classically trained pianist, and proud father of two young boys. Mr Rogers currently resides in San Diego, CA, USA.

ACKNOWLEDGEMENTS

The authors would like to acknowledge the legions of practitioners, consultants and academics worldwide, whose collective contributions provided the foundation for this work. Without their efforts, the practice of Information Technology Service Management (ITSM) would not exist, nor would its chief framework, the Information Technology Infrastructure Library® (ITIL®). In creating this work, we have truly stood upon the shoulders of giants.

The authors would also like to acknowledge itSMF USA, including the officers, staff and volunteers who do so much to help promote ITSM as a professional discipline.

We would like to thank the following reviewers for their helpful suggestions: Brian Johnson, CA, Chris Evans MBCS DPSM - ITSM Specialist, Dave Jones, Pink Elephant, and Roger Williams.

Finally, the authors would like to acknowledge Ms Michele Esposito, whose quiet voice of inspiration and keen eye for detail were instrumental in creating this work.

CONTENTS

Table of Contents

INTRODUCTION

You're probably asking yourself, "Why another book on ITSM?" The question is legitimate. A cursory glance at the IT Governance bookshelf will reveal a wealth of material on ITSM and its accompanying framework, ITIL®.

We undertook the challenge of writing this book because, while there is a plethora of material about the underlying mechanics of ITSM, we found very little advice on how to implement ITSM best practices to achieve an organization's business objectives.

The official ITIL® volumes do an excellent job of explaining what service management is, how the various processes should work and fit together, and why IT shops are wise to adopt the practice. However, the books are notoriously vague on how to design and implement a working ITSM model within a real-world organization.

In times of fiscal austerity and hard-budget constraints, it is imperative for organizations to transform enterprise IT by breaking down silos, consolidating infrastructure, and moving towards a flexible service-oriented architecture and enterprise-shared service model. For example, the United States Navy, one of the largest organizations in the world, has publicly stated its goal of reducing business IT spend by 25% over five years through enterprise IT efficiencies[1].

Figure 1 depicts the clear industry and government trend away from owning assets and managing infrastructure (fixed-cost) to procuring and managing on-demand (variable-cost) services. But there is an inherent trade-off involved: capturing cost efficiencies requires the development of capabilities to manage a service-provisioning environment that is more difficult and complex.

---

1 *http://www.doncio.navy.mil/CHIPS/ArticleDetails.aspx?ID=3568*.

Introduction

Anyone who has developed a service level agreement (SLA) for a multi-sourced Cloud service knows what we are talking about.

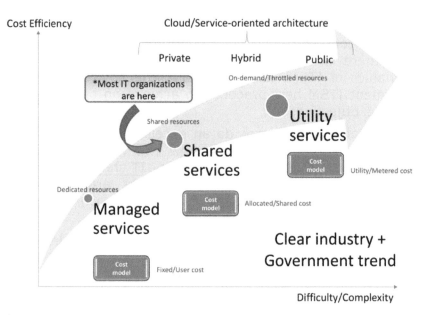

Figure 1: Transformation of enterprise IT

Developing the organizational capabilities to efficiently and effectively manage enterprise IT is what ITSM is all about, and is an essential component of any IT Transformation journey. But what is the optimal approach in an enterprise where multiple business units are moving at different speeds and with different objectives? How do you convince warring factions to work together toward a common strategy and objectives? How do you structure incentives to encourage good enterprise decision making and optimize return from the organization's investment in IT capabilities and services?

The practice of IT Service Management is rapidly gaining traction around the world, and for good reason. Regardless of the size of the firm, or the market it serves, IT professionals can no longer ignore the rapidly growing tsunami of companies adopting a service management approach, both internally and externally. In short, ITSM enables IT to achieve its *prime objective*: the provisioning of high-quality services to the Business at optimized cost, with an acceptable level of risk.

While there is tremendous value in adopting practices from complementary frameworks, we suggest that ITIL® provides the logical foundation and best "running head start" for most organizations seeking to transform enterprise IT; and why not? The framework covers nearly every aspect of the information technology world in an integrated and easy-to-understand manner.

Yet, despite ITIL®'s growing popularity, organizations seeking to "adopt and adapt" ITSM best practices continue to struggle with practical implementation, and in justifying the time and money spent. After all, many organizations and their IT departments more closely resemble dysfunctional families than Max Weber's[2] "Ideal Type," Few, if any, are immune to the enervating effects of organizational politics, personality conflicts, misaligned incentives and entrenched interests – with which we are all painfully familiar. We believe the issue is not due to any lack of merit or utility in the framework, but rather in its practical implementation in the real-world arena, where bottom-line results are all that matter.

We find also that, too often, practitioners seek to apply an academic model to a real-world situation, only to find that the solution is sometimes worse than the original symptom. When that happens, management grows disenchanted, users become dissatisfied, and clients begin to find more suitable firms with which to do business. Obviously, no one wants to be part of such a bleak development, and yet,

---

2 *http://plato.stanford.edu/entries/weber/*.

more often than not, that outcome is all-too-often the rule rather than the exception. If ITSM is such a good idea, and ITIL® such a good framework, why do IT professionals continue to struggle? One obvious answer is in the adopted approach.

In our travels, we have met many ITSM practitioners, all of whom express the same set of common complaints:

"I can't seem to get traction on this (i.e. ITSM) in my company."
"This all sounds good, but where do I start?"
"How do I convince my CEO / CFO / CIO (pick one or more) to back this?"
"How do I get the staff on board with this? They think it's just a lot of overhead."

These questions, and many others like them, are why we have decided to write this book. The Ten-Step approach outlined in these pages makes no claim of being a magic solution, nor the definitive end-all, be-all to enabling IT Transformation. Far from it. Rather, it outlines a tried-and-true approach that provides practitioners and users with a structured, yet flexible, method for achieving ITSM success. This logical step-by-step approach – grounded in common sense and good business practice – has worked for us in a variety of settings over the past several years.

In this volume, we offer tips and techniques, make recommendations on what to do and what not to do, and reference a series of templates we have developed that can be customized to fit any organization's model and appetite.

We would like to believe our approach covers every detail and contingency, but we are too practical and experienced for such delusions. No one has all the answers. We are certain we'll hear from readers with ideas and a recommendation on how to make this approach even better; and that is great. Your feedback is not only welcomed; it is also strongly encouraged. The ITSM community can only grow stronger when its members share the best of what they have learned, and alert the rest of us not only to a better way of doing things, but also to how to avoid the pitfalls that may be encountered along the way.

That being said, we firmly believe our approach is *at least* an 85% solution. This methodology has been used in firms both large and small, and across a variety of industries – including government agencies.

Our approach recommends ways in which the reader can tackle specific issues, and offers advice and guidance on the potential pitfalls and obstacles typically encountered, including tight budgets, unsympathetic staff, and resistance to organizational change.

In our combined 30 years of experience helping companies improve their ITSM practices, we have consistently observed **Four Keys** to achieving ITSM success. We strongly recommend keeping these recommendations in mind, and referencing them frequently, as you journey through each of the Ten Steps:

1. **Avoid the "big bang" approach:** ITIL® is specifically designed as a framework for achieving incremental and continuous improvement, not overnight results.

2. **Establish Executive sponsorship:** ITSM Transformations commonly fail to deliver the desired value due to lack of planning and support from executive leadership.

3. **Invest in required resources:** ITIL® is a long-term investment in the transformation of the management of IT. Many organizations fail to make the required investments in infrastructure, tools and personnel.

4. **Manage organizational change:** ITIL® is a strategic initiative that must be embraced by both business and IT management. ITSM transformation requires detailed workforce planning and the hiring/retraining of key personnel.

Who should read this book?

First and foremost, this book is intended for our fellow practitioners and consultants that have taken up the ITSM cudgel, and charged into battle, only to find themselves outflanked by misunderstanding, indifference, or outright hostility. We hope this book will be particularly helpful for those who have gained some measure of traction, but who are now finding that progress is slowing to a crawl, or has completely stopped.

We who have taken the courses, passed the exams, and then tried to apply the academic lessons to the real world know that knowledge alone is a *necessary*, but ultimately *insufficient*, condition for ITSM success. Knowledge must always be tempered with hard-won practical experience, and the wisdom that ensues as a result of that experience.

Secondly, this book is intended for IT Directors and C-suite executives charged with the responsibility of transforming the role of IT into a value-creating business partner. They will want to read this book (and perhaps mandate its use) to help establish a service management culture and drive necessary improvements in their respective organizations.

Finally, we are very excited by the rapid growth of service management as an academic discipline, and believe this book to be a valuable contribution to the growing body of literature on the subject.

In closing, remember that this Ten-Step approach will be no better and no worse than the time and effort that you, the practitioner, put into it. This book offers a roadmap, and describes a set of tools with which to design and implement the capabilities that will benefit your organization. However, the real work of forging the right relationships, educating management and staff, and of building strong coalitions to support your efforts belongs to you and your team. Good luck!

CHAPTER 1: SETTING THE STAGE

The curtain rising on the opening night of a Broadway production is, perversely, the final step in the process of actually producing and presenting the performance. Prior to that opening night, the producers, directors, actors, stage hands, carpenters, lighting technicians, and dozens of others worked long hours to ensure that all items were taken care of, and that no detail was overlooked. Each person – regardless of whether it was the director, producer, or playwright – broke the action down into its component parts, examined them, tweaked them, reworked them, and then repeated the process all over again until they were satisfied they had the best possible production.

While that was taking place, carpenters were busy constructing sets, Foley artists were painting background landscapes, and set designers were arranging the furnishings and props in a way best conducive to the play's action unfolding on the stage. Electricians, costumers, caterers, accountants, and a host of other staff – some permanent, some temporary – worked in tandem to stage what each hoped would become Broadway's next smash hit.

What does this have to do with Information Technology Service Management (ITSM)? It has everything to do with it. If you think about it, the two activities are very similar to one another. Preparing an organization to take on a service management mindset takes the same amount of energy, preparation, and coordination as staging a Broadway production. The people involved in ITSM aren't called producers, playwrights, or directors, of course. Instead, their titles are Project Manager, Process Analyst, Service Owner and ITIL® Subject Matter Expert, but each person – regardless of the part he or she plays – must understand their role, must execute it in the context and timing of the larger production, and must work with the other members of the team to ensure that the firm's service offering (whatever it may be) satisfies the vision articulated by the senior business sponsor.

As an ITSM practitioner, you will be required to wear many hats, and perform many different (albeit related) functions. As you work through the steps outlined in this book, be mindful of the specific role you're assuming. Some days, you'll take on the responsibilities of the producer or director; on others, you'll be called upon as a stage hand. Knowing the role you're playing on any given day is essential to keeping your ITSM production on track. Not only will it provide you with a laser-like focus on what must be done, it will help to clarify the inevitable discussions that will take place, and the conflicts that will arise. That being said, let's get started.

Let's assume the client is a mid-sized insurance carrier headquartered in the United States. It is a privately-held firm, but one whose activities are managed by a very active Board of Directors. They have recently embarked on an aggressive five-year plan that includes modernization, acquisition and expansion. The Chief Executive Officer (CEO) has been with the company for 15 years, rising through the leadership ranks until assuming his current duties six months ago. To support his efforts, the CEO has assembled a strong, knowledgeable and seasoned management team. This team is intimately familiar with the insurance business – its pitfalls and potential benefits – but has only a rudimentary working knowledge of how IT can help them achieve the Board's long-term goal – to expand the firm's national footprint, and thereby increase market share. The firm has a fairly substantial amount of cash on hand, and is willing to spend a reasonable amount in order to improve operations to the point where taking on a 25% increased book of business is possible. Senior management's collective opinion is that current IT operations would be unable to sustain services should volume significantly increase.

A prime responsibility of a Broadway producer is to secure funding for the production. Money, as the old adage goes, makes the world go around. Your ITSM transformation initiative is no different from any other project vying for the company's limited pool of money. In order to successfully compete for your share of the pie, you'll be required to show how your project will contribute to the bottom line. Don't make the mistake of assuming that everyone will automatically understand how improving ITSM practices will produce a return on investment (ROI).

Despite the fact that ITSM has received a lot of press, and favorable word of mouth, to many people it's still a vague and mysterious "dark art." Given that frame of mind, you'll have to present – to the CEO and your colleagues – convincing arguments for why a share of the firm's precious dollars should be funneled to you. A well-crafted business plan will give the Board confidence in your approach, and will help to win over those skeptics that may exist in your organization.

To you, of course, the answer is obvious. ITSM will enhance efficiency, improve services, and generally make life better all the way around. While this may be true, quantifying those qualities may prove difficult. So how does one go about building a convincing Business Case?

Note: Even though you may have the full backing and support of the Board of Directors or Chief Executive Officer, it is always a good idea to put together a well-structured business plan. Depending on your particular circumstances, more or less attention may be given to specific sections of the plan, but, regardless of your situation, you'll want to have a business plan to fall back on. It's good insurance.

Appendix A contains a Business Case template that we have found useful. We have also developed a Cost-Benefit Analysis workbook that can be used in conjunction with the Business Case template. These tools, if used together, can help you present a compelling argument.

On its surface, the Business Case template looks rather complex, but closer examination will reveal that it contains not only the justification for financial investment, but also the beginnings of your operational roadmap (discussed in greater detail in Step Six). The Business Case will include a clear statement of executive sponsorship, expected financial benefits (tangible and intangible), total financial costs, non-financial benefits and costs, and a risk analysis (which should include the risks associated with executing the project, as well as those associated with not doing so). And while it is not mandatory, an analysis covering the expected organizational impact that will result as a consequence of your ITSM initiative is strongly recommended.

Within the business plan, you will lay out several possible approaches (courses of action). A good rule of thumb is to present as least three viable options. This shows leadership that you've thoroughly thought through the challenges and obstacles that may be encountered, and that you have a firm grasp on how to circumvent or avoid them.

The ancient Chinese warrior Sun Tzu observed, "Many calculations lead to victory. Few calculations lead to defeat." The more scenarios you can envision, and anticipate, the greater your probability of success. In addition, you'll instill confidence in your audience that you can handle any circumstance that may arise (even if it's not wholly anticipated). Your selected approach will spell out all the reasons why you've decided on your selected course of action, and why leadership should support it. This portion of the Business Case will undergo the closest scrutiny, but if you've done the necessary legwork, you'll be able to deftly answer any questions or concerns that may be voiced.

Notice that for the selected approach you will list assumptions and known constraints, projected milestones (with corresponding deliverables), lay out the critical factors necessary to your (and the company's) success, and highlight critical dependencies.

Before moving on, we'd like to take a moment to discuss assumptions and known constraints, as this is an important topic that is often misunderstood.

Assumptions are simply that. They are scenarios that you, as the preparer of the Business Case, assume to be true at the time the Business Case is created. If these assumptions prove to be incorrect or non-existent, the implication is that something in your Business Case **must** change. The same holds true for known constraints. If identified constraints are removed or modified, then something in the Business Case **must** be altered. This must be clearly and completely understood, not only by you, but also by your audience.

The implications are obvious. Imagine you are undertaking a journey by car, and have mapped out a specific route. You estimate that it will take you eight hours to complete, and cost you the sum total of $250 for fuel, food and tolls. You have a known constraint in that you have a total budget of $300, with no opportunity to procure additional funding. You also assume that the road on which you plan to travel is accessible. If that constraint and assumption holds true to form, you have no problem. You may proceed according to plan.

Imagine, though, that due to unforeseen weather conditions, you're forced to take a detour that takes you 50 or 100 miles out of your way. Your original plan is now at risk. (Some would say unredeemable.) You can no longer complete the journey in the planned eight hours, and there is the very real danger of running out of funds, possibly stranding you short of your destination.

The assumptions and known constraints in your business plan, if changed, will have a similar effect on your transformation effort that the unexpected detour had on the scenario described above. Therefore, a prudent ITSM practitioner would be wise to periodically revisit the business plan to ensure that one's assumptions still hold true, and that the known constraints haven't changed.

Of course, if assumptions and known constraints have changed, that will form the basis of the intelligent conversation you can then have with the business sponsor on alternatives. Knowing the impact that the changed assumption or constraint will have on the project, you can then suggest one of the other courses of action in order to get the project back on track.

Another key component of the business plan is your proposed execution plan. This isn't the detailed roadmap you'll lay out in Step Six. This is the *Reader's Digest* condensed version. It lays out the execution approach (phased implementation, targeted approach to address critical pain points, etc.), specifies planning assumptions, talks about potential technology impacts, and offers a high-level estimate for required resources. This analysis needs to be detailed enough to be 80% accurate, but doesn't need to drill down to the Work Breakdown Structure (WBS) level. Ideally, this approach will be detailed enough to give the sponsor confidence that your project will come in within 20% of the proposed budget and schedule. Because it is an estimate, you'll need to revisit this aspect of the implementation with the sponsor as the project plan becomes more detailed.

An important point we'd like to stress here is that the execution planning assumptions are not the same as the overall assumptions mentioned earlier. The former assumptions dealt with the implementation at the macro level. They addressed assumptions concerning overall efficiency, the company's strategic vision, and the impetus for undertaking this effort in the first place. The execution planning assumptions should focus on matters that would (if realized) derail the project. This includes issues such as having the right mix of personnel assigned to the implementation, ensuring that they have the required blend of skills and experience, and they will be committed to the project for the requisite time to complete the tasks to which they are assigned.

Another key section of this document is the risk management plan. Any change introduced into the organization carries some measure of risk. That is the nature of the beast. However, don't assume that all risk is bad. Risk can be beneficial if managed correctly. This section of your proposal must identify all the potential risks that you believe may arise. More important than that is how you (or the company) plan to mitigate those risks. An approach that's acceptable for an innovative start-up may be completely inappropriate for an established, conservative firm. It is up to you – as the key ITSM subject matter expert – to assess your firm's risk appetite, and to tailor your mitigation plan accordingly.

Organizational change management is covered in far more detail in Step Seven of our approach. That section deals with the importance of organizational roles and responsibilities, and discusses the various ways in which you can foster required change through the organization. And make no mistake about it – adopting a service management model is a significant organizational change. Unless your organization is already committed to a complete service management philosophy, transforming the practice of ITSM is going to change the way you do business, and will have a direct impact on the internal workings of the organization. Your challenge in the business plan is to alert the sponsor that a cultural shift is going to take place, and to give them some idea of the work required to effectively manage it.

Before discussing the next section, a point of clarification is in order. The IT Governance Institute defines **governance** as "… the leadership, organizational structures and processes that ensure that the enterprise's IT sustains and extends the organization's strategies and objectives."[3] We acknowledge – and agree with – this definition. However, a full-blown discussion of enterprise governance and all it entails is beyond the scope of this work. For our purposes, we would like to concentrate our focus on the control

---

3 *COBIT 4.1 Framework, Control Objectives, Management Guidelines, Maturity Models*, IT Governance Institute (2007).

objectives an organization should put in place in order to ensure its strategic objectives are being realized.

Last – but certainly far from least – the business plan lays out the expected benefits. Although it comes last, it is the section that will receive the most scrutiny and questioning. Therefore, it is critical that your analysis takes into account **all** relevant factors.

There are a variety of methods for building the best case, worst case and most likely scenario models, each with their individual strengths and weaknesses. We have no preference for which benefit model the reader chooses to use, and will, therefore, offer no recommendations. What is critical, however, is that the expected benefits satisfactorily answer the following questions:

1. Is the proposed plan adequate? Does it accomplish the intended objective within the business sponsor's guidance and parameters?

2. Is the proposed plan feasible? Can it be accomplished within the established time, cost and resource limitations?

3. Is the proposed plan acceptable? Does it balance cost and risk with the advantages to be gained, and meet the requirements specified by executive leadership?

4. Is the proposed plan complete? Does it incorporate the activities and tasks that must be performed to achieve the outlined objectives?

5. Does the proposed plan reduce costs, increase revenue, improve efficiency, or achieve some combination of the above?

If you can answer "yes" to all of the above, then you can have every expectation of your plan being approved and funded by the business sponsor and, at the same time, you will have taken a very big step toward success.

Your Business Plan is done – now what?

Even though you now have an approved business plan, and have received the requisite funding, you still aren't ready to move on to the next step. One more crucial bit of preparation is required. You now have to communicate – to the rest of the organization and to your external business partners – what you are planning to do.

This is important for two significant reasons. The first is that it sets the foundation for your future organizational change management efforts. Secondly, it offers you the opportunity to educate everyone about ITSM – what it is, what it does, and what the expected benefits will be.

Many people in the organization will assume that ITSM is simply another management fad – quickly implemented, quickly forgotten – that is doomed to ultimate failure. Others will see it as a boon – the answer to all their organizational prayers. The majority of staff will fall somewhere between these two extremes. Their approach will be to "wait-and-see." Depending on their perception of your ITSM initiative's success or failure, this group of people will either embrace the service management mindset or reject it completely.

This is natural and expected. It takes time and energy to bring people around to a new way of thinking and a new way of doing business. Organizational change – no matter how ultimately beneficial – is never easy. In fact, we view this step as so critical that we have devoted an entire chapter to it. Remember that you are the principal cheerleader for ITSM, and it is your responsibility to effectively manage this change, and ensure that the proper "tone at the top" is established.

In order to do so, one of your first orders of business after leadership approval is to arrange awareness training and education. Even if staff in your company *think* they know what service management is and what it entails, it can't hurt to provide a refresher course. For those who have heard about ITSM, but haven't taken the time or effort to learn more about it, these educational sessions will come as an eye-opener.

Formal training sessions offer several benefits. They:

- Foster organizational awareness: Even those staff not directly involved in your transformation initiative will learn what you are doing and what is planned and an educated staff is a better performing staff.

- Establish a common lexicon: Most often, in projects such as these, the new nomenclature becomes a source of confusion and ambiguity. Formal training sessions, augmented with pocket glossaries distributed after the sessions, allow everyone to speak the same language, and eliminate the "Tower of Babel" effect.

- Provide context: Staff – especially at the lower levels – often do not know or understand the rationale behind projects of this scope and nature. Training sessions are an excellent way of showing them how this will positively affect their day-to-day responsibilities.

- Ensure historical and documentary continuity despite staff turnover and organizational realignment.

- Encourage active participation: A good training program is designed not only to teach, but to motivate and engage. The right training partner will help plant the seeds of future champions willing to support your cause.

Some clients insist that all personnel achieve – at a minimum – ITIL® Foundation certification. Personally, we don't feel this is necessary. Unless people are going to assume process or service-oriented roles in the organization, the anxiety of having to study for – and pass – the exam, is more stress than the results are worth.

Everyone should be trained, everyone should understand what the new service management culture will mean to the firm and the way in which doing business under this model will affect their day-to-day responsibilities, and everyone should be supportive of the effort. Everyone, however, does not need to become an ITIL® Expert.

At the conclusion of the training, staff should have a clear understanding of how to:

1. Execute activities and tasks consistently using standardized processes.
2. Manage expectations (between peers and supervisors) predictably.
3. Achieve clear visibility of outcomes and standard metrics.
4. Analyze and improve processes that are "built to change".
5. Avoid process failures.
6. Improve and clarify their roles and responsibilities.

This level of preparation will seem daunting to some. To others, it will be seen as being too slow. Often, companies adopt ITSM because they have specific pain points they want to address, and they want those issues resolved immediately (if not sooner). In some cases, you will have been brought in to perform a "quick turnaround."

We want to say this in the strongest possible terms: **don't shortchange the planning process!**

Tactics without a clear-cut strategy are simply sound and fury, signifying nothing. A strategy without well-designed tactics is nothing more than an academic exercise. A comprehensive strategy will direct and guide your tactical efforts. Feedback received from your tactical successes (and failures) will refine and improve the strategy. One cannot succeed without the other. They are the symbiotic sides of the same coin.

Now that we've created the business plan, obtained leadership's approval, been allocated the requisite funding and conducted our education and awareness training, it's time to move on to the second step in our approach: inventorying the current service offering.

To summarize, the actions you want to take in this step are:

1. Draft a creditable Business Plan, complete with:

   1.1 Clear executive sponsorship

   1.2 Rudimentary financial analysis

   1.3 Risk analysis

   1.4 Organizational impact

   1.5 Analysis of alternatives

   1.6 Assumptions and constraints

   1.7 Recommended implementation approach.

2. Offer a proposed execution plan.

3. Identify required resources.

4. Execute a training and awareness campaign.

CHAPTER 2: INVENTORY THE CURRENT SERVICE OFFERING

Via your business plan, you've earned the mandate to consolidate and streamline IT services across the board. Moreover, repositioning IT from cost center to value center opens the door to developing new, value-creating services – provided the ROI justifies it.

It is now time to take the first active step in your ITSM transformation journey. This may seem like a daunting challenge, and it is. The last thing you can afford is to stumble out of the gate. **Step Two** provides guidance on where to start and how to achieve that first critical "quick win."

With the new service model, management envisages not only a significant increase in the number of users accessing our systems, but also expects that the type of user will change. The current customer profile is older (above 45), and content with a paper-based, client/agent system. The targeted demographic is young, computer-savvy, and primarily prefers to conduct business via the web, or through a smartphone application. A younger customer base also implies key service offerings must be available on a 24/7 (24 hours per day, 7 days per week) basis.

In short, our IT services are no longer simple enablers of business process; they are rapidly becoming an *intrinsic component* of our most critical business capabilities. But in order to map a course to the future, we must know our starting point. What assets do we have to work with? How far and fast do we need to travel? Taking inventory of our current service offerings helps us answer these questions.

The following discussion is based on the business profile and organizational goals of the fictional insurance company described in the previous chapter.

More than likely, your firm's profile will be different. Regardless of the backdrop, our approach will allow you to achieve two fundamental objectives:

1. The foundation of a strong, structured Service Management model that can evolve and mature over time.
2. Establishing an organizational mechanism that is nimble, flexible and responsive to the business.

Now that you have your business plan, the $64,000 question is: where do you go from here? What do you need to do over the next 12-18 months to shore up the firm's existing lines of business, establish a foundation for rapid growth and acquisition, and train your staff to deliver and support the firm's services?

In our hypothetical insurance company, the following conditions exist:

1. There is no overall plan controlling IT activities, nor are those activities necessarily supporting business goals.
2. The various IT units do not coordinate activities in any structured or meaningful way
3. Internal requests for service (incidents, trouble-shooting, new requests) come into the Help Desk in a variety of ways (e.g. e-mail, telephone or "drive-bys").
4. External service requests are captured by Sales and Marketing, and are conveyed to IT via the business unit heads.
5. Requests are handled on a "first-in, first-out" basis, and are assigned to resources based upon who is available at the time.

6. Requests are neither classified nor categorized. There is no complete and accurate repository of past requests.

7. Several home-grown applications (Microsoft® Excel® spreadsheets and Microsoft® Access® databases) that were created to satisfy pressing business needs are now supported by IT staff because the original developers have left the firm.

8. Employees are insisting on using personal devices (tablets, smartphones) to access company data and applications, and are in some cases by-passing IT altogether.

The IT department serves four independent business units, each with its own set of specialized needs and desires. Along with Legal, Accounting and Human Resources, IT is a shared service, whose costs are allocated back to the business units by an agreed-upon formula. An 18-month-old audit – performed by an internal team – uncovered several significant exceptions that have yet to be addressed.

Preliminary analysis reveals that IT's priorities are set by the business unit that is either the most vocal, or has the discretionary funds to allocate to new projects. In our scenario, each business unit controls its own profit and loss (P&L), although there are plans to move to a centralized model.

Depending on the organizational and financial maturity of your organization, it may be necessary to educate stakeholders (both IT and Business) on the value of going through this exercise. We recommend conducting an initial kick-off meeting with key sponsors and stakeholders to explain, and hopefully gain agreement on, some basic foundational tenets. *Figure 2* depicts an actual PowerPoint® slide we have used with client organizations, but, of course, the exact messaging should be tailored to the needs of your audience and the culture of your organization:

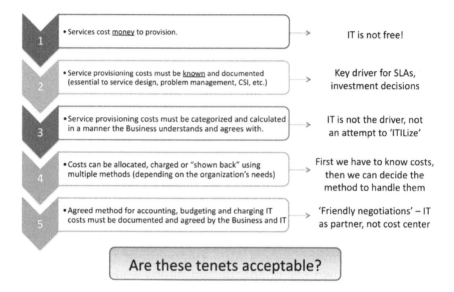

Figure 2: Basic tenets of service costing

When inventorying the current service offerings, it's important to consider all aspects. And by that we mean **all** aspects, including hardware, software, personnel and business partners (internal and external; actual or potential). Don't make the mistake of limiting your field of vision to one or two aspects of your resource pool. The truly effective Service Manager understands that service delivery is composed of many components, and those components are often tied together in a way that is often misunderstood.

Your staff represent the raw material you must work with in order to craft your service management model. Taking an inventory of current activities will provide you with three key pieces of information:

1. The types of activities in which the staff are engaged.
2. The total amount of time spent on those activities.
3. Whether those activities are performed efficiently.

Human capital constitutes one fifth of the five types of assets (the others being Processes, Applications, Information, and Infrastructure) that must be adequately managed. Getting a handle on what those assets are doing today will allow you to make intelligent decisions about what they will do tomorrow.

Many businesses have little to no idea how their resources (human capital or otherwise) are being utilized. Successful resource management is the art of deploying resources – in the most cost-effective way possible – in order to execute and deliver those activities most important to the business. This is especially relevant when new services or requirements are developed and approved. Therefore, the clever Service Management professional will thoroughly analyze and understand the current state of the service model before proposing any changes to it. This is accomplished by:

- Understanding the current resource requirements (this is **not** the same as taking a headcount – this is about understanding how many resources are minimally required for each key activity).

- Collecting and validating existing service delivery documentation.

- Identifying and engaging stakeholders from key functional areas.

- Agreeing on a best-practice process workflow (including frequency, timing, and dependencies).

- Creating – with business input – a standard questionnaire for the current state assessment.

- Deciding whether to conduct one-on-one interviews or group session workshops (questionnaire can be used in either setting, although each type of session should be customized to ensure the best possible response).

- Discussing the results with the business.

IT Services	Labor		Software		Hardware		Hosting Services	Service Fees	IT Mgmt & Misc	Total Cost Individual Services	Percent of Total
	Internal	External	License	Maint	Equip	Maint					
Information Technology Infrastructure and Operations											
Directory Services & Email	510,390	55,000		51,924	14,333	41,693	263,000		68,017	1,004,357	52.52%
Phone/Phone Sys/Voicemail	250,294			29,837	3,583	22,437			24,489	330,640	17.29%
Conf Room Equip & Support		110,000		3,500					10,564	124,064	6.49%
Web/Voice/Video Conf (Ext)	44,067			24,366				350,000	34,937	453,370	23.71%
Communications	804,751	165,000	0	109,627	17,916	64,130	263,000	350,000	138,007	1,912,431	9.16%
WAN/LAN & Internet	487,691	30,000		133,300		88,000		608,400	128,815	1,476,206	47.70%
Wireless Telecomm Services				19,600				1,337,000	129,695	1,486,295	48.02%
Remote Access (Citrix / VPN)	10,134				7,187	873		32,400	9,103	104,344	3.37%
Telecommunications Services	25,571			44,647					2,445	28,016	0.91%
Telecommunications Services	523,396	30,000	0	197,547	7,187	88,873	0	1,977,800	270,058	3,094,861	14.83%
Desktop/Laptop H/W	335,222	165,000		65,480	1,200,250				117,022	1,882,974	72.48%
Desktop/Laptop S/W	32,304		165,000	22,300		36,074			22,177	277,855	10.69%
Personal Printers/Copiers		350,000			52,000				35,182	437,182	16.83%
End-User Computing	367,526	515,000	165,000	87,780	1,252,250	36,074	0	0	174,381	2,598,011	12.45%
Service Desk Operations	216,844	609,000		96,135	7,167	873			88,913	1,018,932	48.70%
Executive Support	354,411								24,323	378,734	18.10%
Event Support	102,823								9,830	112,653	5.38%
Site Support	332,724	180,000							49,018	561,742	26.85%
Service Desk & User Support	18,528								1,771	20,299	0.97%
Service Desk & User Support	1,025,330	789,000	0	96,135	7,167	873	0	0	173,855	2,092,360	10.03%
LiveLink	248,809	196,800		272,306	28,667	43,205			75,506	865,293	39.49%
SharePoint	223,445		65,033			121,000			16,323	425,801	19.43%
Content Management	601,589	132,000		26,290	28,667	33,421			78,009	899,976	41.07%
Enterprise Collaboration Services	1,073,843	328,800	65,033	298,596	57,334	197,626	0	0	169,838	2,191,070	10.50%
Retail Apps	1,523,260	515,500		318,583	25,083	55,668	375,000		185,479	2,998,573	52.37%
Financial Apps	1,173,351	75,000		391,854	21,500	9,021			159,345	1,830,071	31.96%
Internal Apps	455,918		15,000	323,535	3,583	29,159			69,522	896,717	15.66%
Applications	3,152,529	590,500	15,000	1,033,972	50,166	93,848	375,000	0	414,346	5,725,361	27.44%
Info Security/Risk Mgmt/DR	687,017	384,200	30,000	134,400	14,333	1,747	35,000	0	123,012	1,409,709	6.76%
Business Intelligence	1,226,614	0	0	237,125	57,333	166,319	0	0	157,156	1,844,547	8.84%
Totals	8,861,006	2,802,500	275,033	2,195,182	1,463,686	649,490	673,000	2,327,800	1,620,653	20,868,350	100.00%

Figure 3: IT infrastructure and operations costs by category

25

While gathering and presenting this type of information isn't difficult, it can be tedious, and prone to misinterpretation. This is especially true if your organization isn't in the habit of quantifying the work performed by IT. Therefore, the assumptions that one makes in creating this spreadsheet must be clearly understood by the intended audience, so that subsequent discussions aren't derailed by irrelevant arguments over the data's validity and accuracy.

It is important to note here that while the financial management of IT is beyond the scope of this book, service cost information (both lifecycle cost and unit cost) is an important input to many ITSM processes, including continual service improvement (CSI). Therefore, accurate collection and categorization of cost data in this step becomes a valuable input in later steps, in which we design the ideal target state, create IT strategic and tactical plans, develop enterprise processes, and continuously improve operations, including making investment decisions.

Developing a logical cost categorization schema is especially important. Cost types and categories should be developed that allow all IT costs to be efficiently budgeted, tracked, and either "charged back" or "shown back" to the business, depending on your firm's accounting model. Whether or not IT costs are invoiced or simply allocated as fixed overhead, the business must be able to understand the IT cost structure and discern the value received from IT.

Developing cost types and categories is not something that IT should do independently. Of course, most IT costs will naturally fall into hardware, software, maintenance or operational categories. But to correctly account for all types of costs (e.g. capital/operational, direct/indirect, fixed/variable, etc.) it is essential to work with the organization's finance area to align with corporate accounting standards and budgeting cycles. In fact, we have learned from several client engagements that, often, the *company controller* or a well-placed *budget analyst* can be the service management practitioner's best friend.

When using this model during a recent engagement, we gained agreement – before the data was gathered and collated – on the IT services that were currently being offered. In the example shown, our client consciously chose to differentiate between communications and telecommunications, as that distinction was important to their business model. Your organization may be different.

Our client also decided he wanted to know how many IT hours were being expended on supporting the firm's executive staff, as well as how much time was spent on supporting planned quarterly events. Management felt that IT support of those activities was having an adverse impact on Enterprise Collaboration Services, such as Microsoft® SharePoint®, and their Content Management application. Notice that, although Executive support comprised only 18% of all Service Desk activities, the actual number of hours for VIP support was more than half of that dedicated to the key business function of Content Management – a result that management vowed to change.

The observant reader will also notice that application support was grouped into three major categories: retail applications (i.e. customer-facing), financial (largely supporting the accounting and bookkeeping functions), and internal applications (which were customized applications designed to aid back-office staff in the receipt and processing of claims). These categories could have been further differentiated, as each category contained at least three separate applications. However, for the application category, our client was content to gather costs, as shown. Again, your organization may feel differently, and may want to know how much it costs them to operate each service. You, as the ITSM practitioner, must help management define how they want to "slice the pie." A banking operation, manufacturing firm or non-profit organization will have an entirely different set of objectives.

For this engagement, quantifying costs for software, hardware, hosting services and service fees wasn't difficult. Those costs were taken directly from the Finance department's records. Their accuracy and completeness was assumed, although we did spot-check a few of the items to ensure there were no hidden costs. Note that while we assumed the records were accurate, we made no assumptions about whether the corresponding services were **needed**. We held all judgment in abeyance, preferring to validate their worth with the business units.

The categories that proved most problematic were *Labor* (internal and external) and *IT Management & Miscellaneous*. Because of the factors described earlier (incomplete and inaccurate record of staff hours spent on services), we were forced to conduct interviews to determine the number of hours to allocate to each service within a specific category. With management's input and acquiescence, we arrived at a fully loaded average hourly rate for the entire IT staff, and then multiplied that rate by the estimated hours derived from the interview sessions with the staff. While this wasn't an ideal situation, it satisfied our need to establish operating costs for each agreed-upon category.

IT Management hours were derived through interviews with the CIO and his direct reports. When the spreadsheet was created, and initially reviewed, it was understood by all concerned that those numbers would be "fuzzy," and would be refined once the firm began tracking actual hours.

Whether you feel this level of estimation is necessary or not is up to you and your business sponsor. We want to stress, however, that inventorying the current service model, with costs detailed enough to provide an actual assessment of the service's worth, is essential.

This baseline is what you will use to validate the current service model with the business unit leaders.

Congratulations! You have taken an important step in your transformation journey, and hopefully created a "quick win" that has helped build stakeholder confidence in your approach to IT service management

To summarize, the actions you want to take in this step are:

1. Gain agreement on current service offerings.
2. Develop cost types and categories.
3. Quantify the cost of each service.
4. Interview key stakeholders.
5. Validate findings with the business sponsor and stakeholders.

CHAPTER 3: VALIDATE THE CURRENT SERVICE MODEL

In terms of the ITSM Lifecycle, as defined by ITIL®, the first three steps in our approach fall under the Service Strategy phase. The Board's articulation of its five-year plan has defined the market it wants to enter, and has set broad objectives for its management team to achieve. The business plan has refined that broad objective by drilling down to a level where the firm can quantify how current dollars are allocated and spent, allowing us the ability to conduct a true cost-benefit analysis.

Validating the current service model – deciding what is to be retained, what is to be developed, and what is to be jettisoned – is another important step in defining the service strategy for our organization. **Step Three** ensures that all relevant stakeholders have an opportunity to define the specific service requirements necessary for each to achieve their desired objectives.

Validation is critically important, and should not be shortchanged or overlooked. Your mandate might be to clean house and "do whatever it takes" to implement a full-scale service management model, but that doesn't give you free rein to impose an arbitrary service model on the organization. The business leaders – subject matter experts in their own right – are the ones best suited to defining the model that will work best for them. Your job is to help them design that model in the most flexible, cost-effective and efficient way possible.

Your first critical step is to develop a list of whom to consult in your organization. In our experience, it's simply not enough to say we are going to "engage with the Business." Everyone pays lip service to "business and IT integration," but how many organizations have actually achieved this? We need to be deliberate and methodical in deciding whom we meet with, and our specific objectives for each meeting.

Choosing the right set of "validators" is both a practical and a political exercise. Yes, we need to capture good, accurate information from those in the right position to provide it. But we also need to be cognizant of, as one client not so delicately put it, "who's who in the zoo." Choosing the right people can build confidence with our executive sponsor and create broad-based support, even to the point of creating *change champions* for our effort. However, choosing one wrong individual with an influential axe to grind can quickly stall the entire effort.

As a starting point, we recommend selecting a balanced set of candidates from each of the following three areas:

1. **Executive Management and Business Unit Heads**: What are the key business drivers (e.g. vital business functions) for the enterprise, and for each business unit? What is the perception of IT? What does the business need from IT that it's not currently getting?

2. **Business Process Owners, Product Managers and Finance**: How do current IT services enable and support key business processes, products and services? What IT services provide little or no business value? What is the current and future funding model for IT services, e.g. enterprise shared services, business unit budgets, percentage of revenues, etc.

3. **Customers, End-users and Technical Staff**: Which IT services are critical to getting the job done? What do you need from IT that you don't get? Which services are the easiest – and most difficult – to support from a technical, staffing and cost perspective?

In our opinion, face-to-face, one-on-one interview sessions are the best setting for this exercise. Schedule at least an hour (preferably two), and meet in a location where interruptions can be kept to a minimum. If you feel the business leader will be agreeable, encourage them to include key members of the staff. Often, these middle-tier managers provide insights that would otherwise not come to light.

The decision to use a pre-determined list of questions or adopt a less formal, free-form discussion is strictly up to you. Of course, we suggest using the approach with which the interviewee is most comfortable. Either method, if properly administered, will satisfy the requirement. The important thing for you, the practitioner, to remember is not to influence or guide the conversation.

When discussing the current service model with the business, you should be in receiving mode only. It is permissible to ask clarifying questions in order to fully understand an ambiguous point, but one should be cautious about expressing an opinion on the state of the current environment. Use the service and cost spreadsheet developed in Step Two as a tool to guide a frank and unbiased dialogue about service value.

Your primary goal is to determine how current services impact business operations (both positively and negatively). Ideally, this should be performed as a 360-degree cross-functional assessment, as IT's impact on different functional areas can vary widely. The last thing you want is to recommend discontinuation of a service based on the opinion of one department, and later discover another department relies heavily on that same service.

Once this understanding is achieved, it's time to take the next step and do a deeper analysis. This may require circling back with some of the same people previously interviewed; that is ok – it will help them see the value in the information they have provided. The goal of this analysis is to *decompose* each service into its value-creating components, identify any redundancy, waste, or opportunities for improvement, and then *recompose* each service as part of a holistic and revamped service portfolio.

To facilitate this outcome, we recommend classifying each IT service and its value components (utility and warranty) into the following categories:

1. **Truly essential** ("must haves"): the service underpins or is an essential component of a key business capability (e.g. an underwriting algorithm, regulatory reporting software).
2. **Value-added** (customer "delighters"): the service is not essential, but creates value through increased revenue, reduced costs, or increased customer/employee satisfaction (e.g. a self-service portal, a free online rate comparison tool).
3. **Marginal or no value** ("expendables"): the service is obsolete, ineffective, or too costly to provide the desired value (e.g. a company-issued Blackberry, an older RAS application).

Truly essential services must, of course, be retained, and usually provisioned in house as a core IT competency. However, these can still be analyzed for improvement opportunities. Value-added services warrant closer scrutiny. Are they actually providing the full value expected, and on a cost-justified basis? These services are always candidates for being redesigned or analyzed for possible cost savings, including outsourcing. Finally, services that are clearly not delivering the desired value should be quickly discontinued or replaced with a service that better meets business needs.

In one of our engagements, the client organization had a very strong Six Sigma culture. Knowing this, we used a Critical-to-Quality (CTQ) Tree to translate the voice of the customer (VOC) and voice of the business (VOB) into rank-ordered requirements for the desired IT services. This approach was advantageous in that it eliminated a lot of the posturing and shuffling for position usually associated with competing departmental priorities. Lean Six Sigma, in particular, is an incredibly focused and agile method for facilitating the kind of quantitative, data-driven approach that helps remove the politics from decision making.

Your organization may have a predilection for COBIT®. If so, your interviews will likely proceed more smoothly than in an organization with little or no knowledge of the tool. COBIT® tells you *what* must be done. ITIL® tells you *how* to do it. Under the COBIT® framework, once the pain points have been identified and prioritized, it is then a matter of mapping the appropriate ITIL® processes to the problem that must be solved, and placing the right controls in place. If this is the path you decide upon, you will be happy to know that COBIT® has already done much of this mapping work for you. The publications are available to members through the Information Systems Audit and Control Association (ISACA®) website.

Regardless of the culture, or how you engage the business leaders, you must ask probing questions. Ask about the current services' good points. Find out why they add value. Ask what would happen if those components were removed or modified. Discover how those beneficial aspects could be/should be improved. How much would the business leader be willing to spend to see an x percent increase in functionality? What is the expected payback period? How much organizational disruption (in terms of staff re-training) is acceptable/unacceptable? If cost wasn't a factor, what three things would the business leader like to see implemented?

The organization has decided to implement a service management culture because they feel the current environment isn't conducive to its long-term goals. The obvious implication is that the current service environment is universally disliked. You may be led to believe that current activities have little or no value. Don't fall into the trap of blindly believing all the bad things (or, for that matter, all the good things) that you hear about the current environment. People tend to gloss over the good, and exaggerate the bad. It's human nature. It is your job to objectively assess – through careful, skillful questioning –

what is truly useful, and what can be changed or eliminated outright.

Take the organization's pulse. Meet with the line managers. If time and money allow, meet also with the line managers' staff. You may hear something unexpected. For every ten people you interview, two will be perfectly happy with the status quo, and will see no reason to change it. Two others will rip it to shreds, and provide 100 reasons why it should be scrapped – in its entirety – immediately. The other six will fall somewhere between these two extremes. This type of unfiltered feedback is not information that can be obtained from the Board of Directors or the CEO. Line managers may complain about the impact IT has on the bottom line of their P&Ls, but that doesn't necessarily mean they want the service spigot turned off. They simply want to receive value for the money being spent.

This is when the service and cost spreadsheet becomes your biggest ally. In our spreadsheet, the overall manager in charge of retail applications may not have realized that he was being charged $375,000 in hosting fees, and a little over $318,000 in annual maintenance. Your interview session with him or her is the perfect opportunity for you to have a frank discussion about the hosting service contract. Listen to the business leader's ideas and suggestions for how to reduce cost or improve the value received from the service. This is the type of proactive engagement you want. Line managers very often feel they have little or no choice in the services that IT delivers to them. Use this opportunity to explode that myth by empowering them to offer solutions that will work for them.

Now that you have successfully engaged with the right stakeholders, and completed an in-depth service analysis, it is time to return to the macro view and formulate the recommended service portfolio. There are two tools we have found especially useful for this effort: the Enterprise Services Heat Map and the Strategic Prioritization Framework.

The *Enterprise Services Heat Map* is a simple, but powerful, tool that is used to map IT services and systems against key business capabilities and processes. When we presented an ITSM Transformation Workshop in 2011 at the *itSMF Australia LEADit Conference*, the heat map generated more interest than any other tool.

Figure 4 shows an example of an actual heat map developed for a multi-line insurance carrier. Because this company operated multiple independent business units, each with its own P&L, the first step was to develop a heat map for each business unit. Then, the individual heat maps were summed together to present an enterprise view.

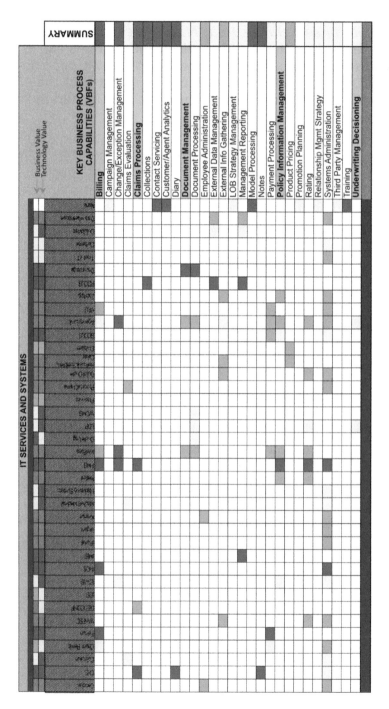

Figure 4: Enterprise Services Heat Map

The diagram depicts IT services and systems across the top (names are shaded in the example), and each is assigned a color code (green, yellow or red) to indicate its relative overall business value, as well as its technological value. These are experience-based value judgments that serve as a key for assigning the detailed color codes in the section below the service names. For example, a service may not directly impact the business, but it may be a key component of the overall technical infrastructure, ensuring that other critical services are operated effectively. This service would score white (N/A) for business value, but green for technology. The reverse may also be true.

The right side of the diagram consists of the key business capabilities and processes, or vital business functions (VBFs) of an organization, listed alphabetically or grouped into logically related modules. These represent the functional elements of enterprise architecture (EA), and, in this example, consist of all the primary operational functions of a typical insurance company: *billing*, *claims*, *underwriting*, etc.

To complete the heat map, a green, yellow, or red value is entered for each instance where a service supports a business function. Green indicates the service fully supports the business process and is providing the desired value. Yellow is a cautionary signal that the service may be suboptimal and could be improved. Finally, a red value indicates a serious gap where the service is simply not providing the level of support required by the business.

Once all values have been entered, the final step is to complete the summary column on the right. The heat map is a qualitative tool, and, therefore, there is no mathematical formula involved; again, this is a judgment-based exercise. If a business process is fully supported by a sufficient number of IT services, it is coded green. On the other hand, if a business process suffers major IT capability gaps, it is coded red. Yellow is assigned to any service/process combination that falls in the middle range.

You will notice that the summary column in this example contains a large number of red and yellow values – a strong indicator of serious IT capability gaps. There is good reason for this – this company was preparing to embark on a major Business and IT Transformation program that included a multi-year IT investment campaign. As the organization gradually transformed its operations and introduced new IT services and platforms, many of these reds and yellows turned to green.

While the heat map helps identify the areas where IT needs to improve, it does not prescribe a solution. In today's economic environment of fiscal austerity and hard budget constraints, very few organizations have the unlimited capital and resources to improve IT in the way they would like. Therefore, executive management must be prudent and deliberate in how they choose to invest their limited capital. The *Strategic Prioritization Framework* is a useful tool for guiding IT portfolio investment decisions.

Figure 5 shows a fictional chart that visually maps potential investment projects three-dimensionally, according to the following criteria:

- **Investment type** (y-axis): what type of IT investment does the opportunity represent – is this a baseline investment, an opportunity-based investment, or an investment in Research and Development (R&D)/innovation?
- **Enterprise strategy alignment** (x-axis): how well does the investment opportunity align with the organization's enterprise strategy (overall impact to all business units) – low, medium, or high?
- **Investment size** (z-axis): what is the relative size and risk of this investment, indicated by the size of the circle? A larger circle indicates higher capital and higher resource and opportunity costs, as well as higher risk.

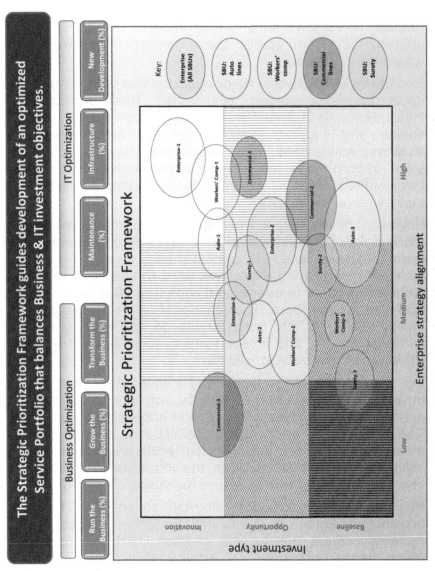

Figure 5: Strategic Prioritization Framework

Unlike the heat map, this chart does not sum individual business unit data. It should display the highest-ranked IT investment opportunities from each business unit, as well as opportunities understood to be enterprise-wide or enterprise funded. This allows an unbiased analysis of all investment opportunities from across the organization, regardless of where they originate.

Executives will naturally favor opportunities that fall into the upper right-hand quadrant of the chart. These projects offer investments in future-focused technologies that directly enable and support execution of the firm's enterprise strategy. Additionally, most executives will favor medium-sized opportunities, as smaller opportunities are seen to have limited potential returns, and oversized projects may be viewed as too risky.

However, developing a truly optimized portfolio requires a more balanced perspective that takes into account long-term business and IT optimization criteria. From the business perspective, executives need to ensure IT invests a sufficient amount of operational capital to effectively *run the business,* but no more. The remainder of the budget should, ideally, be split into investments to tactically *grow the current business*, and investments to strategically *transform the business* over the longer term.

Everyone these days believes IT should be "run like a business," so, naturally, IT has its own internal targets for optimal levels of operational, tactical and strategic spending. One of the CIO's primary responsibilities is to fund enough *maintenance* to keep the lights on, while ensuring sufficient capital and resources to keep the *infrastructure* upgraded, and *develop* or migrate to future technological platforms.

Helping your organization smartly govern its IT spend according to agreed business and IT spending targets will do more to cement the success of your ITSM transformation effort than almost any other activity. If your organizational culture and budget allows, this is an ideal time to bring in a consultant with expertise in IT strategic planning. A skilled consultant will be able to help the executive team benchmark values against industry peers and competitors, and set appropriate targets to achieve its long-term goals.

In Step Two, you collected current IT service and cost data, and took steps to understand service demand. In Step Three, you have validated your results with the right stakeholders, and performed a detailed service value analysis. The end result is stakeholder agreement on an optimized service portfolio that includes future investments.

This, of course, is the true value of Service Management – facilitating outcomes customers want to achieve without their having to take on the ownership of specific costs and risks. By working together, you can collectively collaborate to reduce costs and improve services. As a result, the business leaders will have a better understanding of the resources it takes to support their particular line of business. In return, you will have earned their trust and respect, and that is a win for everyone.

On paper, this step is the easiest to describe. In practical terms, it is one of the most challenging. It involves becoming part educator, part sounding board, and part whipping boy. The end result, though, will be allies who support the Service Management implementation. The line managers are either going to be advocates or adversaries. If you're going to be successful, you want a lot of the former, and very, very few of the latter.

To summarize, the actions you want to take during this step are:

1. Identify and engage with key stakeholders across functional areas.

2. Develop a needs/services questionnaire jointly with customer representatives.

3. Decide on a "best means to an end" – i.e. conduct one-on-one interviews, or facilitate group workshops.

4. Agree and document business value-based, rank-ordered IT service requirements using a tool such as CTQ Tree.

5. Analyze results and develop Heat Maps and service maps.

6. Discuss results with the business, highlighting cost/trade-off areas.

Now that the current state assessment is completed and the findings discussed with your peers, it's time to establish a governing body.

CHAPTER 4: ESTABLISH AN ITSM STEERING COMMITTEE

In our experience, **Step Four** – the founding of an ITSM Steering Committee, authorized to oversee the design and implementation of the service management model – is the single most critical component of this entire process. Composed (as it should be) of business unit leaders, IT representatives, and subject matter experts, this body will be responsible for dealing with service and process design issues, and for adjudicating and rendering decisions that must be reached, compromises that must be negotiated, and risks that must be mitigated. Used effectively, the members of this board will facilitate and enforce standardized service and process design, testing, and deployment activities. They will also be a key stakeholder in all operational issues that may arise, as well as sponsoring and governing all improvement initiatives.

When assembling this board, there are a number of critical matters that cannot be overlooked or minimized. In fact, we feel so strongly about them that we refer to these tenets as the "Ten Commandments" of organizational IT governance.

1. Ensuring cross-organizational representation: this means including members from all areas of the organization – from Finance to Operations to IT.

2. Writing a charter that clearly spells out the Committee's responsibility, scope of authority, and primary objectives.

3. Defining (at the initial session, if not prior to that) the Committee's procedural operations (e.g. who will serve as Chair; how voting will be conducted, and under what circumstances; what constitutes a majority; etc.)

4. Outlining specific procedures for handling exception requests, non-concurrence, and points of order, including veto rights and decision escalation.

5. Widely communicating (to relevant staff **and** executive leadership) all Committee decisions.

6. Defining and enforcing enterprise service and process standards, including interoperability.

7. Adjudicating disputes between key ITSM functions and roles (e.g. service owners, process owners, stakeholders, suppliers, etc.)

8. Prioritizing, funding and orchestrating enterprise service and process improvement opportunities.

9. Establishing a completion timeframe and set of deliverables for each stage of the ITSM Lifecycle[4].

10. Including a "sunset provision" to force periodic evaluation of the Committee's performance, and to allow removal of the Chair or complete dissolution of the Committee if it fails to achieve its chartered goals.

While, in theory, all "Commandments" should carry equal weight, we feel the last one is the most important for ensuring the long-term success of your transformation effort. People change roles; political winds shift; organizational priorities change. In addition, the very act of implementing new or changed service management practices will transform the organization. Some changes will be large; others small. Yet, each one will alter the organization's dynamics. The ITSM Steering Committee must stay attuned to this nuance, manage it effectively, and evolve with it, as need be. For all of these reasons, it is

---

4 This topic is covered in more detail in *Step Eight: Define a Standard Process Development Approach (Chapter 8)*.

strongly recommended that Committee members periodically review and update the Committee's actions, mandates, scope of authority, and responsibilities.

Not only must the Steering Committee evolve with the organization it serves, it must also be held accountable for its performance. Unaccountable Committees are anathema to service management success; if the Committee fails to achieve its chartered goals within a reasonable period of time (for any reason), deliberate action must be authorized and taken. This may require intervention from a higher authority, for example the CIO or CEO, which is why executive authorization for the Committee must be clearly enumerated in the charter. We do not achieve ITSM success by crowning or coddling ineffectual regimes.

The key to an effective charter is to ensure it contains all the elements necessary for the smooth, efficient operation of the Committee. In our opinion, the charter should include the following sections:

- **Background:** for clarity's sake and to provide historical context, it's desirable to state the conditions that necessitated the Committee's creation.

- **Purpose:** this statement clearly and unambiguously declares the reason for the Committee's existence.

- **Scope of authority:** this defines the parameters of the Committee's authority.

- **Goal:** this establishes the broad goal or goals the Committee is intended to accomplish.

- **Objectives:** the quantitative or qualitative steps that will lead to achieving the stated goal or goals.

- **Membership:** this states, by name or title, the Committee's members. This section may also declare the role each member is expected to assume on the Committee (e.g. Chairperson; Secretary).

- **Procedures:** this section details how the Committee's business will be conducted. It typically contains procedures for defining what constitutes a quorum, and includes steps for how to call and conduct official votes, and how decisions shall be rendered.

- **Meeting frequency:** this defines the frequency of Committee meetings, and may also include a section on how to call ad hoc sessions, if necessary.
- **Communication:** this specifies how Committee minutes, decisions, action items, etc. are distributed to affected personnel and relevant stakeholders.
- **Duration:** if time-bound, this dictates the term of the Committee's existence.

Note: It is strongly recommended that all charters contain a built-in expiration date. This forces the organization to perform an active review of the Committee's purpose, goals and objectives. Committees with open-ended durations often lose their focus after a year or two of existence, especially if not chaired by a strong, forceful and visionary personality within the organization.

Once the charter has been drafted, and has passed its internal review, it needs to be endorsed – in writing – by the CEO or the CEO's designee. This legitimatizes the Committee and gives the body more weight and authority. Ideally, you'll want a permanent Secretary/Facilitator to ensure consistency of action from one session to the next, and serve as the Chairperson's adjunct. Minutes should be recorded and maintained in a public (i.e. web-based) library that will serve both as a historical reference and ongoing operational resource for new employees, as well as those unfamiliar with the original conditions necessitating any decisions rendered by the Committee.

In the course of executing its mission, the Committee will be required to render decisions and adjudicate disputes. Decisions made in this forum **must** be communicated as widely as possible. This point cannot be stressed strongly enough. In our opinion, one of the primary reasons that ITSM improvement initiatives fail or become delayed is a lack of communication. Either decisions are not conveyed to those on whom it will have the greatest impact, or the information is incomplete or inaccurate. Change is difficult enough when everyone understands what needs to be done. Don't unnecessarily complicate matters through poor or non-existent communication practices.

There are a variety of ways in which decisions can be publicized. Experience has shown that a standard format works best. An effective communication mechanism offers several benefits. It:

- Alerts the organization that a decision has been rendered; this is especially true if the decision is entered into a database or content management system that automatically generates messages to specific groups that are established within Active Directory®.
- Presents the decision in an easy-to-understand format (see provided example).
- Provides people with a point of contact for questions or concerns regarding the rendered decision.
- Minimizes confusion and ambiguity.

Figure 6 depicts a communication mechanism that has worked particularly well for us.

ITSM Steering Committee Notice of Decision (NOD)	3/29/2010
A Notice of Decision issued on behalf of the ITSM Steering Committee	

Decision ID:	
Identifier:	
Notice title:	
Notice date:	
Effective date:	
Affected group(s):	
Decision:	
Basis for decision:	
Impact/Actions:	
Contact:	
Sponsor:	
Standard distribution:	
Additional distribution:	
NOD approved by:	
NOD approved date:	

Figure 6: Notice of Decision (NOD)

As can be seen, the Notice of Decision (NOD) is structured to allow an organization to assign an internal numbering / document identifier scheme for inclusion into a Content or Knowledge Management Database System (KMDBS). This allows staff the ability to search for, and retrieve, information about decisions rendered by the ITSM Steering Committee. When properly used, the NOD acts as an effective communication mechanism to all affected staff and relevant stakeholders.

Note: There will be instances when rendered decisions may have to be modified or reversed. This is normal, and shouldn't be viewed as "waffling." Changing circumstances (either internal or external) will necessitate a change in direction. In fact, failing to adapt to surrounding conditions when circumstances dictate that you must is both foolhardy and destructive. Should this situation arise in the course of your project, simply issue a new NOD that clearly explains why the previous decision is no longer applicable, and reference the outdated NOD in the new distribution, so that readers will understand what has changed and why. Not only is this good business practice, but it will develop in the staff the habit of consulting the NOD library.

The effort involved in putting together an ITSM Steering Committee of this nature shouldn't be minimized or underestimated. More likely than not, the people you'll most want to have as members of your Committee will decline to serve, either because they will be "too busy" performing their day jobs, or because they will secretly feel unqualified. If they've attended the training and education sessions you were foresighted enough to arrange, the prospective members will have a good working knowledge of ITSM, but they won't (with a few possible exceptions) be experts. They'll want you – as the ITSM professional – to take charge, chair the Committee, and make most of the major decisions.

As flattering as this may be to you personally and professionally, don't accept the assignment. You're an ITSM professional, not a business leader. ITSM exists to enable and support the business; the cart should never be placed in front of the horse. Although it may seem counter-intuitive, it is actually in your own best interest to allow (or force, as the case may be) the business to make the decisions that drive the strategy, design, development and implementation of ITSM best practices. Business representation on the ITSM Steering Committee is a must. It not only ensures that IT capabilities meet business needs, wants, and concerns; it also has the added advantage of continually educating the Committee members on ITSM's benefits.

This is where the selection of the ITSM Steering Committee Chairperson becomes critically important. The person at the head of the table has to have enough "*gravitas*" within the organization to lend the proper air of authority to the Committee – especially during its formative period. The Chair needs to be high enough in the organizational hierarchy to compel the attendance and full participation of the other members. Assigned action items won't be addressed in the stipulated timeframes unless the action item owner knows he or she will be taken to task if the item isn't addressed. The Chair is ultimately accountable to the CEO. The Committee members must be ultimately accountable to the Chair.

An ITSM Steering Committee with a weak Chairperson is as ineffective as a Committee with no genuine authority or organizational responsibility.

It's a good idea to attend the first several ITSM Steering Committee meetings. You can coach the members through their duties and responsibilities, as well as answer any tactical questions not clearly addressed by the charter. You can be the Committee's support, and spiritual leader, but it is up to the Chair and other members to make the Committee an effective body.

What you want to avoid is having a Committee comprised of members who are afraid to make decisions. While agreement is ideal, not every decision will be met with universal approval. It is impossible to please all of the people all of the time. What the Committee must strive for are decisions that have a positive effect on the largest number of people, or a decision that achieves one of the organization's strategic goals. In your role as observer and mentor, it is your responsibility to alert your business sponsor – or the ITSM Steering Committee Chair, if that's a more appropriate course of action – if it becomes evident the Committee is ineffective. It may be difficult or uncomfortable to broach the subject, but failing to do so is a risk to your project and to achieving your objectives.

If you are faced with a situation like this, your best course of action is to document the pitfalls of the Committee's failing to render a decision. Within the corporate world, frame the discussion in terms of potential revenue loss. If you work for a non-profit organization, talk about the failure to serve the targeted constituency, and the negative publicity that will result. Be as objective as you can, but never fail to be honest and straightforward. The organization will be better served for it.

In many organizations, other committees or working groups already exist that will exert influence upon – or be influenced by – the ITSM Steering Committee. Two examples we commonly encounter are Architectural Review Boards and Risk Management Boards. If these exist, ensure these committees and working groups are intimately aware of the progress of your ITSM efforts. Ideally, a representative of the ITSM Steering Committee should be a participating member in those other groups. By engaging with them early in the process, you ensure they have advance notice of potential changes affecting their respective areas. Face-to-face communication is the best form of communication, and this is best accomplished by cross-seeding members of the various groups with a stake in your ITSM initiative into the ITSM Steering Committee, and vice versa.

If other formal committees or working groups don't exist in your organization, the Steering Committee Chairperson should assign a member to establish and oversee those ancillary boards. A prime example of this is Risk Management.

All new initiatives have inherent risks and opportunities. Responsible leaders (like you) seek to minimize the former and maximize the latter. This means that someone must actively assess the potential risks and opportunities, and craft plans to address them. Identified risks and opportunities should then be assigned to an individual tasked with its care and administration. If no one person is held accountable for crafting an effective mitigation or execution plan, the organization may find itself taking on more risk than it can comfortably handle. Conversely, opportunities will not be fully exploited unless someone actively seeks to take advantage of them.

One final note must be made here. While the broad topic of enterprise governance is well beyond the scope of this book, its importance cannot be overlooked. Suffice it to say that, whatever form and structure your Steering Committee takes, it must align with the organization's enterprise governance model. For example, the ITSM Steering Committee may need to be established as a subsidiary body beneath the organization's top-level IT Steering (or IT Strategy) Committee. Unfortunately, enterprise governance is not widely discussed or understood in many organizations; therefore, it is imperative that the CEO, as conduit to the Board, understands and endorses the role the ITSM Steering Committee is tasked to perform.

The opposite may also be true. Many larger organizations, particularly in the financial services area, have established mature enterprise governance models that already incorporate a service management governance body. One example that is growing in prominence is the Service Management Office (SMO), or IT Service Management Office (ITSMO). Alternatively, many organizations have established either a Process Owner Council or Service Owner Council – or both. These may or may not report to a higher-level governance body. If either case is true of your organization, then your challenge is to either structure the ITSM Steering Committee to align with these existing entities (while avoiding overlapping authority), or, more likely, to modify and/or reconstitute these authorities to ensure that the

Steering Committee goals discussed in this chapter are achieved.

As previously stated (and as will be stated again), implementing a Service Management model will change the organization's dynamics. It is important to recognize, and plan for, the inevitable changes in both organizational structure and employee job responsibilities, as well as changed interaction between departments.

The ITSM Steering Committee is the organizational "brain" of your Service Management implementation. Therefore, its care and feeding should be paramount among your priorities. Neglect it at your own peril.

> In summary, the actions you want to take in this step are:
> 1. Assemble an ITSM Steering Committee with cross-organizational representation.
> 2. Draft a charter outlining the Committee's role, responsibilities, and scope of authority.
> 3. Educate the Committee members on their duties and areas of responsibility.
> 4. Formalize a standardized, repeatable communication strategy, and use it consistently.
> 5. Create a repository for housing and maintaining a historical record of Committee decisions and issues.
> 6. Ensure the ITSM Steering Committee is properly aligned with the organization's enterprise governance model, including other groups with which it must interact.

Congratulations! You are now ready to leave the Service Strategy phase of the Lifecycle and enter Service Design.

CHAPTER 5: DEFINE THE IDEAL TARGET STATE

The steps described thus far logically fell under the Service Strategy phase of the ITSM Lifecycle as defined by ITIL®. The Business Plan, including the analysis of alternatives and the selected course of action, outlined the broad activities the organization wanted to undertake in order to realize its articulated goals.

Inventorying the current service model provided much-needed insight into the state of the environment, along with an understanding of the true costs involved. Assessing the current model also offered insight into the environment's strengths and weaknesses.

Chartering and creating the ITSM Steering Committee established an authorized and accountable group of business-oriented stakeholders, whose primary function is to provide guidance and support during the planned implementation of ITSM best practices.

Via the Board's / CEO's vision statement and long-term goal setting, the organization's strategy has been articulated, codified, and finalized. The ITSM Lifecycle will ensure that feedback from the Service Design phase through to the Continual Improvement phase will hone and refine the strategy, but, for now, we will consider the Strategy phase of the Lifecycle to be complete.

Steps Five through Seven of the Ten-Step approach cover activities that logically fall within the Service Design phase of the Lifecycle.

When designing a new building, the architect assesses a myriad of factors: the land on which the building will be erected; its planned use when completed (i.e. residential, commercial, or a combination of both); the components required to erect the structure; local regulations and building codes; environmental concerns; future use; and so on. There are a host of activities and tasks that must be considered before the first shovel overturns the first clump of earth. So must it be with defining the organization's ideal target state. We have said it before, but it bears repeating: **don't make the mistake of acting before planning!**

Strategy without tactics is an idea that will never be realized. Tactics without strategy is wasted time, money and opportunity. There are countless case studies where service management initiatives failed simply because the organization lacked a coherent, strategic plan, supported by relentless tactical execution. You do not want to have your organization become a member of this sorry club.

After much debate, we ultimately decided to include the diagram shown in *Figure 7*, below, which depicts the core elements of a strategy and the relationships between them. It may seem elementary and self-evident to most of you, but we have discovered a surprising number of people who confuse these basic concepts. For example, if people in your organization use the terms "goals" and "objectives" interchangeably, you may wish to use this diagram to educate them.

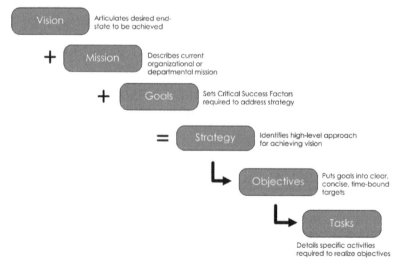

Figure 7: Strategic components

At the highest level is the organization's vision. It articulates the desired end-state that is to be achieved. It represents where the organization wishes to be five, ten, or fifteen years in the future. This is the culmination of the journey upon which you are about to embark. The organization's vision is cast in stone and should rarely, if ever, change.

The organization's mission statement describes the essence of what it does – its purpose for being. Like the vision, the mission provides long-term continuity and is not easily changed. The Coca-Cola® Company publishes its mission statement on its website. In its entirety, it reads:

Our Roadmap starts with our mission, which is enduring. It declares our purpose as a company and serves as the standard against which we weigh our actions and decisions.

- To refresh the world …
- To inspire moments of optimism and happiness …
- To create value and make a difference.[5]

There is no ambiguity in this mission statement. It states clearly and concisely what the company does, and why it exists. Your mission statement should be equally compelling.

Goals are the third variable in this equation. They set the critical success factors (CSFs) necessary to address the articulated strategy. A good example of a strategic goal is:

increase the number of policyholders by 15% by the end of the next fiscal year.

---

[5] *www.thecoca-colacompany.com/,* July 13, 2012: *http://www.thecoca-colacompany.com/ourcompany/mission_vision_values.html/.*

This goal is specific, measurable, attainable, realistic and time-bound. It is a SMART goal. The goals set by your Board of Directors, CEO, or senior leadership must be as clearly articulated as this. Otherwise, those tasked with realizing the goal will have no discernible way of determining whether they were successful or not. Strategic goals are typically longer-term in nature (one to three years), but, unlike the vision and mission, they are subject to change and should be updated as required, based on changing environmental factors. If your organization does not already have a strategic planning methodology, we highly recommend Porter's Five Forces[6] as a time-tested approach to assessing an organization's strategic environment.

As can be seen in *Figure 7*, the vision plus the mission plus goals comprise the organization's strategy. The strategy identifies the high-level approach to achieving the desired vision, while ensuring that the current mission is continually carried out. This last criterion is especially important. After all, if you can't keep current operations going, eventually you won't have an organization or corresponding culture to improve! The strategy should be set according to the organization's strategic planning cycle (typically three to five years), and periodically revisited to ensure alignment to the current environment.

Once the strategy has been agreed, it must be operationalized. This is accomplished by breaking down strategy components into discreet, measurable objectives. Objectives decompose the strategy into manageable units of work that are constrained by specific timelines, which have deliverables attached to them.

In almost all cases, tactical objectives should be associated with one or more key performance indicators (KPIs), which are aligned to higher-level goal-based critical success factors (CSFs). Objectives are like mile markers on the freeway –

---

6 *http://en.wikipedia.org/wiki/Porter_five_forces_analysis* (September 30, 2012).

tactical indicators letting us know if we are going in the right direction. Well-defined objectives should be relatively stable, but can be updated when required to align to changing tactical conditions.

Finally, objectives themselves are further decomposed into a variety of tasks that detail the specific units of work required to realize the objective. Tasks should be defined with care and precision, as they become the crucial link between disparate activities across the enterprise. Tasks are by definition operational in nature, and should be updated or changed as often as required to achieve the objective. Never lose sight of the objective, or the strategic goal it supports.

Note: Most firms are content to track progress at the task level. However, there is another school of thought that maintains that work should be tracked at the detailed work instruction level. Adherents argue that work instruction-level tracking provides a more accurate estimate of time and effort. We don't agree with this line of thinking, but acknowledge that this methodology has its advocates, and is practiced – albeit rarely – in the business environment. In our opinion, the cost of tracking progress at the work instruction level outweighs any potential benefits that may be gained. Tracking effort at this level of detail is tedious both for the person actually doing the work, and for the line manager, who must gather the information and consequently summarize it for senior management's review. An alert, well-trained project manager should be able to manage progress and cost at the task level, with no detrimental impact to the overall plan.

The CEO and executive team have laid out long-, medium-, and short-term goals and expectations. You've taken those goals and expectations, and used them as the foundation for the work that must be completed. You have repositioned IT as a value-added business partner, and identified the key IT capability gaps in the current environment. During your validation of the current service model, the business leaders have provided their wants, needs and desires. The result of that analysis is a rank-ordered list of requirements. In that rank-ordered listing is the assumption that required changes to the IT architecture and supporting infrastructure are included. If that isn't the case, then those requirements should be added to the list to ensure you have a comprehensive catalog in hand. In Step Five, every single one of these requirements will go into designing the desired target state.

Before continuing, let us stress that this is **not** the time or the place to address expenditures – potential or otherwise. Until this exercise has been completed, adopt a cost-agnostic approach. Budget and resource trade-offs will be addressed later on. At this point, the sole objective is to design a target state that satisfies the requirements that you've captured. For the purposes of this exercise, assume an unlimited budget.

When defining the target state, you'll want to define the following primary components:

1. A detailed description of the key process characteristics required to support business activities.
2. A definitive listing of new, improved or modified capabilities.
3. A set of relevant management control practices.
4. An agreed-upon method to measure success.

The approach used here is similar to the one used in the current state assessment. Using the ITSM Steering Committee as both a sounding board and resource, you'll want to determine the key interfaces and dependencies between the various factors supporting and delivering services. Determine the functions, organizations and workforce necessary to support the target state. Which are the key capabilities that should be retained in house as core competencies, and which are candidates to be sourced from suppliers, partners, and/or the Cloud? Take note of any assumptions made during this design stage. Assumptions are supported by beliefs, not facts. Should the facts conflict with beliefs, the activities and tasks associated with that assumption will have to change. This is where the greatest risk resides, and is usually the place where most ITSM Transformations go off the rails. Once documented, people are extremely reluctant to abandon their assumptions, even in the face of all evidence to the contrary.

The primary deliverable from this step is what we have termed the "IT Ecosystem©." An ecosystem is typically defined as "a community of living organisms (plants, animals, and microbes) in conjunction with the non-living components of their environment (things like air, water, and mineral soil), interacting as a system. Ecosystems come in various sizes but usually encompass specific, limited spaces. Ecosystems are defined by the network of interactions among organisms, and between organisms and their environment."[7] The coined phrase "IT Ecosystem" illustrates how the business and IT processes – and the people who interact with them – are dependent upon one another to deliver service to the customer, and thereby provide value to the organization.

Figure 8 represents one example of the deliverable that was produced for a client engagement. This dynamic model of people, processes and technology working functionally together to produce specific outcomes the customer wanted to achieve served as the basis for building out the service management system for this organization. The reason the model worked so well is that it was both intuitive to the client, and structured to address the practical needs the client himself had identified. In short, the model reflected

---

7 *www.wikepedia.org*, July 14, 2012: *http://en.wikipedia.org/wiki/Ecosystem*.

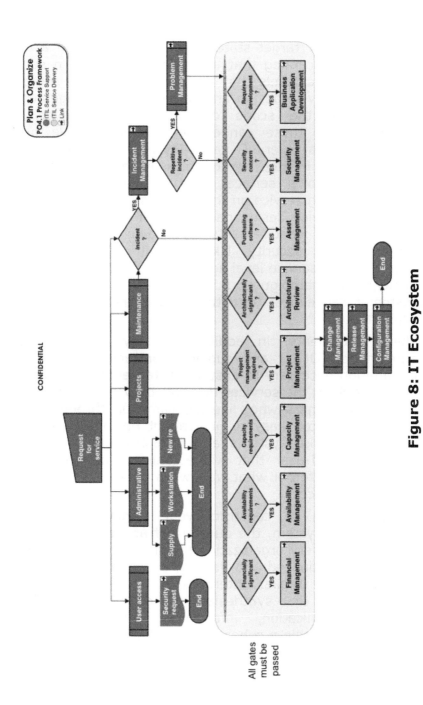

Figure 8: IT Ecosystem

The single most important step towards ensuring the success of your target state design is to establish a user-facing service catalog that accurately defines each service and the service levels that will be supported. A complete treatise on service design and service level management is well beyond the scope of this book; however, the importance of these cannot be overlooked. We highly recommend that every IT capability and future investment priority agreed in Step Two be formally chartered as part of the organization's service portfolio. Furthermore, every customer-facing service on the business catalog should have a detailed service design package (SDP) that specifies the service level requirements for availability, capacity, continuity and security. Likewise, all orderable services should have a service level agreement (SLA) that expresses, in clear and unambiguous business terms, exactly what the customer can expect from the service, including how it is supported.

These documents, in addition to any operating level agreements (OLAs) and supplier contracts, provide vital information necessary to ensure our target state design will actually deliver the services demanded by the business. For those practitioners who, like us, came up through the IT ranks, it's all too easy to get caught up in the details of processes, tools, systems and infrastructure, and forget about the end-user that will actually utilize the offered service. Never forget what we always tell our clients: *it's all about the services!*

As you begin to construct your target state service management system, the question of architecture becomes preeminent. Every organization has architecture, whether it is planned, optimized and flexible, or whether it is ad hoc, inefficient and fragile. Enterprise architecture (EA) is the top-level view that synthesizes the organization's various business, application, information, and infrastructure architectures within a coherent set of *Principles, Policies and*

Guidelines to govern enterprise design. EA is analogous to John Stuart Mill's famous Utilitarian Principle[8], in that it seeks to balance competing objectives and design trade-offs to achieve what Mill described as "The Greatest Amount of Happiness Altogether." An optimized EA is one that satisfies current operational needs, while ensuring an agile, secure, and cost-effective platform to support future growth and changes in business strategy.

As mentioned in the previous chapter, many organizations have established an Architectural Review Board or similar governance body. Some organizations even employ a chief architect, who, as you might imagine, wields significant authority and influence. In Step One, we advocated befriending someone in Finance. If your organization has an enterprise architect, we recommend you add this person to your shortlist of friends, and reserve a table for three at your next happy hour. It isn't your job to architect the business, but you better make sure that your service management system is in accordance with your organization's EA principles, policies and guidelines.

There are three basic approaches to EA. First, there are generic reference frameworks, such as TOGAF® and the Zachman Framework™, that can be adopted and adapted to facilitate architectural planning at any organization, regardless of industry. Secondly, there are specific reference architectures designed to meet the needs of an organization within a specific industry. These are often developed by large branded consulting firms – a good example being IBM's insurance industry reference architecture. Finally, some organizations have developed their own proprietary architectural frameworks. A great example that we are familiar with from our work with the United States Navy is the Department of Defense Architectural Framework

---

8 *http://suite101.com/article/the-utilitarianism-of-john-stuart-mill-a63950* (September 30, 2012).

(DoDAF). For anyone who doubts the importance of these standards, DoDAF has a direct impact on how billions of tax dollars get spent every year on IT and weapons systems acquisitions. At the end of the day, EA is the steward for all business capabilities and services that IT must support. For example, the key business process capabilities used to populate the heat map (*Figure 4*) in Step Three were derived from an insurance industry architecture model.

Like any true ecosystem, our interacting components are comprised of many underlying activities. A detailed explanation of the work involved in crafting this system would fill an additional volume. However, a few words on this model's creation are in order.

This model assumes that all requests for service – internal and external – are captured via the Service Desk. As the request is received, it is immediately categorized. This categorization determines the work stream the received service request will follow. Let's say that the initial service request is an interruption in service. The technician receiving the call would immediately initiate the incident Management process, depicted in *Figure 9*.

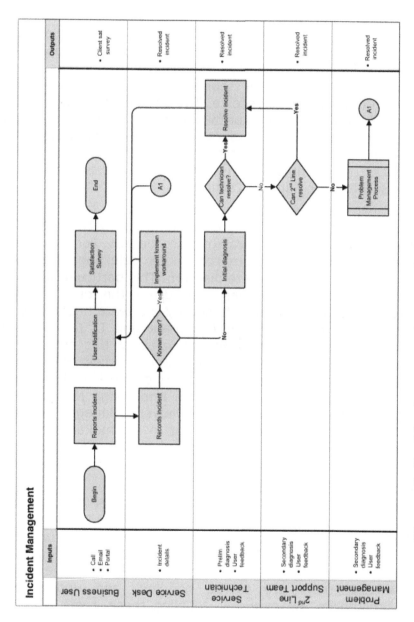

Figure 9: Incident management process (swim lane view)

As can be seen, the Incident Management high-level process shown on the initial landing page of the IT Ecosystem is further expanded to detail the actions that will be taken by the first- and second-tier technicians. By using swim lane-type diagramming, it is simple to graphically depict the primary responsible party, as well as the inputs (data, documentation, remedial steps already performed, etc.) that person is expected to receive. The process diagrams outline what the technician is expected to do, as well as the output they are expected to produce. Should – in this case – the incident have to be escalated to the Problem Management process, this contingency is also noted, and is initiated by the Second-Tier Support Technician.

What can't be shown on this static model are the embedded hyperlinks to all supporting documentation, such as detailed work instructions and escalation procedures. For this client, staff accessed the documentation by selecting embedded links within the appropriate diagram. This particular iteration of the IT Ecosystem was housed on the organization's internal website, and maintained by the team headed up by the person responsible for Corporate and IT Governance. The organization – realizing the value of this structure – made the IT Ecosystem a critical item in their governance hierarchy. In your organization, a model such as this might be owned and maintained by the Knowledge Management Process Owner or the Service Delivery Manager/Director. Whoever this person may turn out to be, make sure he or she is accountable, and is an executive with enough clout to enforce the model's stipulated procedures, and one who can guarantee its accuracy.

While not a Business Process Management (BPM) tool in the true sense of the term, the IT Ecosystem utilizes many of BPMs' most desirable characteristics. It defines the handoffs, timing and responsibilities among the various entities that may be utilized. It takes into account (in 99% of the cases) how exceptions are to be handled, and under what circumstances. By explicitly detailing these items, you will significantly increase staff productivity and morale. In researching ITSM improvement initiatives, Gartner Research has found that organizations who take the time and trouble to document these items achieve productivity improvements of 12% or greater, even without any process redesign.[9]

Ultimately, the maturity of your IT capabilities and supporting processes depends heavily on software-based tool automation. Paper-based processes are at best guides, and ultimately unenforceable; the incentives to find workarounds are simply too high. Leveraging existing tool capabilities, and planning to acquire additional required capabilities in the future, is a critical component of your target state design. The level of automation required by an individual process depends on the process goals, CSFs and KPIs, as well as its interdependencies with other processes. At some point, most service provider organizations will require the advanced management capabilities of a BPM tool (integrated process discovery, design and orchestration). When this time comes, the IT Ecosystem becomes an invaluable source for loading inputs, outputs, data, roles, etc.

The level of detail that this particular client insisted upon may consume more time and effort than your organization is willing to expend. If that is the case, fine. Each organization is different, and has its own immediate needs to address. What we do want to stress, however, is that the relationships between the various processes – business and IT – must be addressed in detail. The reason why Henry Ford's assembly line worked so well was that each person involved in the process knew **exactly** what he or she had to do. Each station along the line knew what was coming, what they had to do with the components (in whatever stage of assembly) when it reached them, and the state of the end product they were expected to pass along to the next

---

9 *Business Process Management's Success Hinges on Business-Led Initiatives*, Gartner, (26 July 2005).

station down the line. This process is no different. We found that Gartner's prediction of increased productivity was well founded. The IT Ecosystem eliminated the guesswork from the decision on whom to engage for any given situation. It fostered communication and teamwork, productivity and efficiency, and – as a result – staff morale improved considerably. Developing a standardized and repeatable approach to enterprise process development is discussed in more detail in Step Eight of this Ten-Step approach.

Lastly, notice in *Figure 8* that the IT Ecosystem incorporates a built-in validation against enterprise and IT architectural standards. The question one must ask oneself is how much of the existing infrastructure can be used to ensure that the various components – business, application, information, infrastructure – work together to deliver required business capabilities and value.

High-performing organizations understand the need for enterprise architectural standards, and actively work to craft a solution that is robust and resilient. They know that genuine value can only be generated when the infrastructure can be scaled up or down to accommodate changing customer demand.

Unfortunately, many organizations pay lip service to this discipline – usually to their detriment. Either they do not understand architecture's importance to the model, or they're unwilling to invest the time and resources necessary to support their long-term goals. When this happens, the discipline very often becomes a source of major contention, and one that – if not properly and adequately addressed – becomes quite expensive.

How many times have you heard colleagues relate stories of a rogue business unit that created a mini-IT department that was totally at odds with the overall structure? Worse, the time inevitably comes when the local hotshot responsible for creating this isolated IT Island inside the business unit will leave the firm. When that happens, responsibility for the maintenance and upkeep of this rogue application will inevitably fall to IT – with disastrous results.

(Typical problems include poor initial design, missing or incomplete documentation, the inability to scale to meet increased demand, etc.)

This situation usually occurs when the IT department is reactive – when it is in constant "firefighting" mode, which is the result of poor planning and inadequate alignment with business needs. Viewed as unresponsive to their needs, the business units seek other service providers (legitimate and otherwise) who can provide solutions to their business problems. Properly implemented and used, the IT Ecosystem virtually eliminates this possibility because it not only accounts for the critical requirements the business unit so desperately craves, it addresses the most critical items in a rank-ordered, planned, and structured way.

In defining the ideal target state for your organization, pay careful attention to the architecture. Leverage its strengths, and minimize its weaknesses. It is the foundation upon which your entire structure will stand.

In summary, the actions you want to take in this step are:

1. Articulate the company's vision and mission statements. If they do not exist, engage your senior leadership and create them.
2. List the organization's strategic goals.
3. If one does not already exist, create an organizational strategic plan that incorporates the ITSM Transformation effort.
4. Define specific, measurable, achievable, realistic and time-bound objectives that will achieve the articulated goals.
5. Plan the tasks necessary to achieve the objectives.
6. Create an IT Ecosystem detailing the interactions and relationships in the target state you wish to achieve.
7. Validate that your service management system:
   a. Supports delivery of target state services and agreed service levels
   b. Conforms to architectural policies, principles and guidelines
   c. Defines interfaces and integration points (people, processes, tools and information).

CHAPTER 6: CREATE THE IT STRATEGIC AND TACTICAL PLANS

Now that the ideal target state has been defined, it's time to roll up the sleeves and get down to brass tacks. **Step Six** is two-fold, and is, arguably, the most difficult step in this entire process. The two primary activities that have to be completed in this step are: agreeing on which of the rank-ordered requirements can be accommodated given the organization's constraints in time, money, and resources; and then creating (or updating) the IT strategic and tactical plans to support those priorities.

The Free Dictionary defines negotiation as "confer[ing] with another or others in order to come to terms or reach an agreement."[10] Even though you have a rank-ordered list of requirements in hand, don't make the mistake of thinking that this will be universally accepted by all parties. Unless the Board or CEO dictates which requirements will be satisfied first (a rare occurrence, indeed!), assume that negotiations will take place.

This negotiation should be largely confined to the business unit leaders that will be most affected by the ultimate decision. If you're dual-hatted (i.e. both an ITSM expert and an IT practitioner with management responsibilities), you should – by all means – fight for your own needs and wants. When doing so, however, make certain that you present your priorities in terms of *business* benefit – either across the enterprise, or in support of a particular business unit. IT exists to service the business, and your best chance of gaining support and advocacy is to show how your requests will benefit the bottom line.

Luckily, when it's time to negotiate, you've had the foresight to create the perfect forum for the exercise: the ITSM

---

10 *www.thefreedictionary.com*, 17 July 2012: *http://www.thefreedictionary.com/negotiate*.

Steering Committee. Composed (as it should be) of representatives from each one of the firm's critical departments, this body is ideally positioned to facilitate cross-organizational dialog, adjudicate disputes, and craft the enterprise priorities that will drive resource allocation, timelines, and deliverables.

Recall that the ITSM Steering Committee was established for this very purpose. As the "brain" of the ITSM Transformation effort, the Committee must be the ultimate decision authority. Charged by the Executive Committee or CEO to act upon the senior leader's behalf, the Committee is responsible (and accountable) for enabling those capabilities that address the greatest number of organization pain points in the shortest time possible.

When initiating this step, be realistic. Unless you belong to one of those rare perfectly performing organizations where every ego is subsumed to achieving the organization's larger goals, this step will require time and energy. It is human nature for people to fight most strongly for what will benefit them first. Although the health and well-being of the organization is paramount, this ideal is often forgotten or overlooked when people begin competing for limited resources.

It is highly possible that the discussions and negotiations will become heated. Tempers may flare. Alliances will form, split apart, and re-form with different members. As much as is possible and practical, let the Committee members voice their priorities and hash out their differences without your input. As the ITSM subject matter expert, your primary role at this initial stage should be to answer questions as they arise, with respect to how specific capabilities can or should be implemented for the particular line of business. Don't forget that ITIL® is a framework, and, as such, it can (and should) be customized to provide the most value for the entity using it. As the discussion evolves, you'll probably be asked your opinion regarding trade-offs, or the feasibility and implication of developing one capability versus another. Answer honestly and without embellishment. Doing so will enhance your reputation as a straight-shooter, and will give the Committee members confidence that you will do what is necessary in order to help them realize the successful achievement of their collective objectives.

As conversations reach the tipping point where key trade-off decisions must be made, you are now positioned to wield significant influence. By wisely holding your ammunition and building credibility with all Committee members, you can now step into the role of an unbiased and trusted advisor, somewhat akin to an internal consultant. Think of this role as analogous to a skilled professional service provider, such as a CPA or tax attorney. Your job at this final stage of negotiations is to help articulate the "art of the possible." Like a complex calculus problem, there are likely an infinite number of combinations of tactical priorities, projects, and resources that can potentially satisfy the organization's goals and objectives. Your job is to expand the "solution space" and help the Committee find an optimized solution to this multivariate equation: a solution that best meets the needs of the enterprise as whole.

Although you must remain neutral in terms of any particular business unit or department, you are anything but an uninterested observer; the success of your ITSM Transformation effort depends on forging agreement on the right set of services, processes, and capabilities needed to get your organization to its desired target state. You can help your cause by articulating solution sets that emphasize the use of *shared services*, *shared infrastructure*, and *common processes* that most efficiently and effectively meet the critical needs of each business unit, while, at the same time, positioning the enterprise to achieve its long-term strategic aims.

If you do your job well, the Committee will ultimately reach agreement on a shortlist of tactical opportunities (new or improved capabilities, processes, services, etc.) that are aligned with the service portfolio and strategic investment priorities determined in Step Three, as well as the target state architecture developed in Step Five. Some trade-offs may require going back and adjusting the portfolio or modifying the architecture of our service management system. That is okay, as long as the enterprise strategy continues to drive tactics, and not the other way around. Step Ten (Balanced Scorecard and Continual Improvement) will establish a formal approach for measuring and reporting our success as we go, which will guide future adjustments.

As a final step, recommendations made by the ITSM Steering Committee should be reviewed and approved by executive management before a final decision is rendered. This step is critical and must not be shortchanged – once tactical priorities are approved, projects will be chartered to acquire or develop the required capabilities to deliver customer requirements. Service design packages and detailed process designs will be created. Service level agreements will be negotiated with customers. Investments in infrastructure will be made. Partner and supplier agreements will be entered into. In other words, once projects get underway, resources are committed, money is spent, and the organization takes on the risk and opportunity cost of the investment. Therefore, this step should be structured as a key decision gate, not merely a "rubber stamp" by leadership.

Note: Once executive management has formally approved the ITSM Steering Committee's recommendations on the final set of deliverables with associated timelines, make sure the Chairperson issues an applicable Notice of Decision. Not only will this serve as your guiding roadmap, it will also provide a written record of the Committee's decision.

Once the negotiations have been completed, and the authorizing Notice of Decision issued, it's time to create the IT Strategic and Tactical plans.

Strategic planning determines where an organization is going over the next three- to five-year time frame, how it plans to get there, and how it knows if it got there or not. Even though the company has already developed its vision statement, and articulated its goals, the planning process provides an opportunity for partners (e.g. business unit leaders) and staff to establish a common language and agreed involvement in the execution of the strategy.

There are a variety of ways to approach strategic planning. Company leadership, culture, the complexity of the goals to be achieved, and the expertise of the personnel tasked with its execution all play a part in how the strategic plan is developed.

Regardless of the approach used, drafting an IT strategic plan has several advantages. It:

- Expands upon the vision and planned approach articulated in the business plan.
- Promotes the effective management of one of the firm's most critical assets (i.e. the IT infrastructure).
- Improves communication between the business sponsor and IT.
- Aligns the strategic direction of IT to the business's function.
- Improves the flow of internal information and processes.
- Helps to efficiently and effectively allocate IT resources.
- Reduces the time span and expense of IT lifecycles, particularly in terms of vendor review, selection, approval, and implementation.

Auditors and Governance practitioners that use COBIT® as their primary tool will find that the Planning and Organization (PO) domain applies here. The PO sub-components of IT Value Management, Business-IT Integration, the Assessment of Current Capability and Performance, the IT Strategic Plan, IT Tactical Plans, and IT Portfolio Management are all principles and control practices that may be applied at this point in the Ten-Step approach.

Your IT Strategic Plan should be a subset of the previously completed Business Plan. While the Business Plan typically addresses a three- to five-year window, the IT Strategic Plan should cover the upcoming 12 to 18 months. We recommend keeping the timeframe confined within this window in order to keep the team focused, and so that short-term achievements can be realized. As we will explore in more detail in the step that focuses on Organizational Change Management, quick wins are essential to sustaining momentum. In addition, most budgets are reviewed (and modified) annually. Therefore, it makes the most sense to align activities to the amount of available funding at one's disposal. In addition, the IT Strategic Plan must link to, and support the achievement of, enterprise goals.

Ask yourself the following questions:

- How can we acquire or develop the capabilities, processes and services mandated by leadership to meet long-term enterprise goals and objectives?
- What does our target state service catalog look like, and what are the critical service level requirements (both service delivery and service support) we must provide for our customers?
- What resources (human or otherwise) are required to support those requirements?
- What timelines (if any) must I meet?

- What are the critical IT functions and infrastructure requirements that must be developed to meet service level agreements and sustain the service management system?

These three legs of the stool – resources, timelines and functionality – are crucial to one's success or failure. Whether you are designing an entirely new service, or merely modifying an existing one, be mindful of the delicate balancing act between these elements. A change to one of the legs nearly always impacts one or both of the others. An unstable stool is useless in the real world. The same can be said of unbalanced service delivery. Deploying a resource after a deadline has passed, or developing a piece of functionality that has no relevance to the business, are both wastes of time and money. It is, therefore, vital that you understand the business needs and drivers, so that you can deliver practical solutions that solve business problems.

In crafting the IT strategic plan, be sure to consider current infrastructure constraints and your organization's long-term architectural roadmap. As shown in *Figure 1*, in the introduction to this book, many Global 2000 organizations and large government agencies are in the process of moving away from owning assets and managing infrastructure (fixed-cost) to procuring and managing on-demand (variable-cost) services. This transformative trend has a significant impact on how IT resources and costs are managed now and in the future. The rapid growth and financial success of companies such as VMware® and ServiceNow™ is testament to the insatiable demand for virtualized, on-demand infrastructure and Cloud-based services. Migrating to the Cloud (public, private, or hybrid) does not change *what* IT must deliver to the business, or the nature of service management. However, trends in server virtualization, software-as-a-service (SaaS), and multi-sourced services certainly affect *how* IT must structure itself to deliver services.

Now that you've successfully facilitated an agreement on the scope and duration of the capabilities to be developed, and the services that are to be delivered, you can revisit the business plan and see what portions of it require updating.

The typical strategic plan consists of nine core elements. They are:

1. Vision / Mission Analysis
2. Objectives
3. External environment
4. Industry environment
5. Internal Analysis
6. Culture and climate
7. Resources
8. Financial Analysis
9. SWOT
10. Choice
11. Action Plan.

Before discussing each element, note that this strategic plan has an IT point of view. Therefore, its focus should be on the strategy the IT department intends to put in place in order to develop the agreed-upon capabilities. Of necessity, it will derive from, and expand upon, the strategic goals articulated by the firm, but every IT goal should support the achievement of one or more enterprise goals. *Figure 10* is an example of IT Strategic Goals supporting business goals.

IT goals linked to business goals

IT strategic goals

ID	
1	Establish enterprise-wide Vendor Management Process.
2	Identify all third-party suppliers and outstanding contractual obligations.
3	Account for and protect all IT assets.
4	Increase security of customer-facing web services.
5	Maintain integrity and accuracy of received client data, and PII.
6	Ensure compliance with laws, regulations, and contractual obligations.

ID	Business strategic goals	Corresponding IT goals		
1	Provide secure website services for customer order submission.	3	4	5
2	Reduce costs to outside contractors / consultants.	1	2	
3	Comply with federal and state regulations relating to personally identifiable information (PII).	3	4	5	6

Figure 10: Goal Linking example

Vision and Mission Analysis

The vision and mission statements in the IT Strategic Plan should be virtually identical to the enterprise's vision and mission statement. It may be slightly modified to make it IT-centric, but it shouldn't stray too far afield from the organization's strategy or business plan. Customization, if undertaken, must tie back to the enterprise's vision and mission statements. Business and IT integration is the Holy Grail of ITSM.

External environment

In our practice, we have used the section on external environment to explore the facets of the project that are outside IT's span of control. This includes not only business departments that are external to, but interact with, IT, but also extends to third-party business partners upon whom IT depends. (An outsourced Service Desk is a typical example of the external environment category. Although contractually bound to deliver services to your firm in a specified way, you have limited influence and control over how those services are delivered to you.) For this category, you would be wise to focus primarily on factors that could potentially derail or delay progress.

Industry environment

The industry environment includes new or advancing technology that may prove beneficial to your strategic or tactical efforts. A new version of a Business Process Modeling (BPM) tool, for example, may be an item in which you want to invest, if it can be proven to improve efficiency or reduce costs. This may or may not have been included in your initial business plan. If it had, then you already have your justification and implied permission to procure the tool. If not, the preliminary analysis should reveal whether it is worthwhile (from a ROI perspective) to pursue the option or not.

Internal Analysis, Culture and climate, Resources

The Strategic Plan's next item – Internal Analysis – is composed of two sub-factors: organizational culture and climate, and resources (human and otherwise). A repeated theme throughout this Ten-Step approach is the necessity of preparing for, and managing, organizational change. This section of the Strategic Plan pulls on that thread a little more firmly. When assessing the culture and climate within the organization, be pragmatic. Don't look at the organization in the way you **wished** it operated. Look at how it, in fact, *does* operate. If your management team believes in building consensus and including everyone in the decision-making process, it would be foolhardy to believe that a unilateral decision by one person will carry the day. An important component of the culture is the climate of the organization. Does the organization believe in taking reasonable risks, or does it adopt a "plays it safe" attitude? This is your opportunity to identify what can be easily accomplished, what may be challenging (but perhaps doable), and what cannot be done given the current state of affairs (e.g. no cultural appetite, insufficient or untrained resources, etc.)

When analyzing resources, account for the human element, as well as the hardware, software and other physical assets that will support your efforts. In the scenario we have been painting to illustrate the Ten-Step approach, a key critical success factor is the firm's ability to rapidly expand capacity to meet expected demand. If you recall, the Board of Directors expects that the introduction of the desired new business service will significantly increase the number of users accessing the web servers. Prudence would dictate ensuring that network bandwidth is sufficient, critical web infrastructure is fully operational, and "hot" backups are available. And while engaged in that analysis, it would also be wise to determine whether the skills and experience of the network administrators responsible for monitoring and maintaining these components is sufficient to the task at hand. Should an incident occur, you'll want assurance that the staff are able to quickly and efficiently resolve the issue.

As mentioned previously, we see many clients responding to resource challenges by turning to public Cloud providers like Amazon Web Services® (AWS®) and Rackspace® to dynamically scale infrastructure and services at low cost. Large government agencies are, likewise, moving in the same direction. For example, the United States Department of Defense (DoD) CIO recently appointed the Defense Information Systems Agency (DISA) as the DoD's "enterprise Cloud services broker" to perform a similar function within the DoD's private (highly secured) Cloud environment.[11]

Financial Analysis

The Financial analysis category – like the vision and mission statements – should be an extension of the approved Business Plan. Where the Business Plan had gross numbers, the IT Strategic Plan should have more granular ones. At this point, given everything you've learned thus far, you should have enough detail to accurately quantify costs in terms of manpower, hardware, software, and potential partner agreements. Unless something unforeseen happens (e.g. assumptions prove to be unfounded, or market circumstances change), the estimates in the Strategic Plan should come pretty close to your actual burn rate.

SWOT

For those readers who haven't been exposed to the term, SWOT stands for:

---

11   *http://www.disa.mil/News/PressResources/2012/DISA-DOD-Enterprise-Cloud-Service-Broker?goback=%2Egde_87778_member_133276821PE*.

- Strengths: those attributes of an organization which give it an advantage over others.

- Weaknesses: those characteristics that place the organization at a disadvantage in relation to others.

- Opportunities: external chances to improve performance in the organization.

- Threats: external elements that could spell difficulty for the organization.

Figure 11 depicts a generic SWOT matrix:

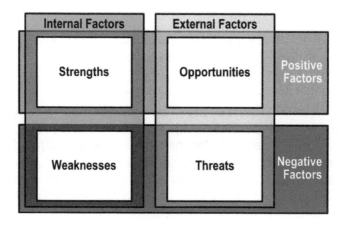

Figure 11: SWOT matrix

Purists argue that a SWOT analysis should be conducted **before** objectives are set. In theory, they are correct. Identified SWOTs are used in subsequent planning process steps for achieving the selected objective. While this is ideal, it is not always feasible. In our given scenario, for example, the objectives have already been established. At this point, you wouldn't want to use SWOT to set new objectives. What you can do, though, is use the results of the analysis to validate that you are maximizing your strengths and opportunities, while simultaneously minimizing your weaknesses and threats.

Regardless of whether this analysis is done before or after setting the objectives, the exercise itself is valuable and shouldn't be discounted.

The aim of any SWOT analysis is to identify the key internal and external factors that are important to achieving the stated objective. These come from the organization's unique value system, and are usually grouped into two main categories:

- Internal factors: strengths and weaknesses internal to the organization.
- External factors: opportunities and threats presented by external entities to the organization.

Note: Internal factors may be viewed as strengths or weaknesses, depending upon their impact on the organization's goals. A factor that is a strength for one objective may be a glaring weakness for another. SWOT is a useful tool when used in the proper context, and with proper understanding, but don't rely on it to the exclusion of other forms of analysis. Consider all viewpoints.

One final thought: when conducting the SWOT analysis, keep in mind that it is specific to the IT Strategic Plan, and does not apply to the enterprise as a whole. Bounding the analysis in this way ensures that you and the team are focused on those factors you can control or influence. Readers interested in learning more about SWOT – its benefits and its deficiencies – are encouraged to consult the representative sources listed in the *References* section at the end of this book.

Choice

Every strategy has several possible avenues through which its goals can be attained. The avenue you select will be the one that is most beneficial in terms of time, money, and effort. If the requisite amount of thought and analysis has been applied to the strategic plan, at this point you will have more than one way to execute it. With two or more alternatives from which to choose, what criteria should be applied to determine which alternative is the best?

For this exercise, we would like to suggest ITSM practitioners adopt an approach similar to the one advocated by the United States Department of Defense (DoD). The DoD stipulates that a Course of Action (COA) analysis be conducted to evaluate possible options for the Commanding Officer (CO) or Senior Executive Service (SES) staff to follow. The beauty of using the COA model is that it forces one to consider whether the recommended options are:

- Adequate: the option must accomplish what the ultimate intention of the CO or SES is.

- Feasible: the option must accomplish the goal or objective within established time and resource limitations.

- Acceptable: the option must balance cost and risk against the advantage that is to be gained.

- Distinguishable: the option must be sufficiently different from other stated COAs.

- Complete: the option must incorporate the objectives, efforts and tasks that are to be performed, and consider the time elements for achieving the stated objectives.

The alternative that best achieves the stated objectives is the one that answers "yes" to the following questions:

- Has the analysis accurately considered and addressed **all** known facts and current conditions?
- Do the results support the achievement of the organization's mission and intent?
- Have all *specified*, implied, and **essential** tasks and their priorities been identified and agreed upon?
- Are all operational limitations (internal and external) known and understood by all relevant stakeholders?
- Does the analysis specify the critical success factors that are necessary to achieve the desired end state?
- Have the relevant measures of effectiveness to show whether objectives have been realized been identified and agreed upon by all relevant stakeholders?

In our experience, we have found that in 99 cases out of 100, *only one* alternative will answer all five questions. That alternative is the course of action that should be selected, as it is the one with the greatest chance of success. The other alternatives will have greater risks.

In the rare case where two alternatives seem equally compelling, let the Business Sponsor select the course of action. As the senior business executive responsible for the success or failure of the improvement initiative, the final decision belongs to him or her.

A financial services client once defined strategy as "the art of knowing what *not* to do." We quite like this definition, as it clearly emphasizes the importance of organizational *focus*. Another definition we like – borrowed from the military, and emphasizing the importance of *leadership* – is that strategy is "the art of the General." Strategy looks at the goals an organization wants to achieve, and decides on the means by which to get there. It is the roadmap the team will follow to ensure the organization's vision is realized.

Action Plan

If strategy is the "art of the General," then the Action Plan – *tactics* – can rightly be called the "art of the Commander." Tactics define an orchestrated set of actions that must be executed in order to achieve strategic success.

Before discussing the Tactical Plan(s) in detail, note that, at an absolute minimum, you should have a one-to-one relationship between the organization's goals and IT's strategic goals. For some enterprise goals, IT may have multiple goals that, taken together, satisfy the larger goal. For others, a simple one-to-one relationship will suffice. Regardless of the situation (i.e. one-to-one or many-to-one), ensure that all organizational goals are addressed. This mapping can serve as the foundation for future presentations you may be required to give to executive leadership or the Board of Directors. It is your proof (and their assurance) that strategic objectives are being properly addressed.

We have long used a Goal Linking matrix similar to the one depicted in *Figure 10*, earlier in this chapter. Note that each one of IT's strategic goals can be directly tied to one or more of the organization's strategic goals. This tight coupling between what the business is trying to achieve, and IT's support of those objectives is critical to the success of both. It is a synergistic relationship that nurtures and sustains both parties.

Of course, each one of IT's strategic goals can be further broken down into smaller sub-goals or objectives. The idea here is to show leadership and personnel that all current and future activities will help realize the organization's long-term vision.

Roadmap

Now that the strategic aspect is settled, it's finally time to develop an implementation roadmap supported by orchestrated tactical execution.

Our recommendation is to assign this task to the best project manager you can find – whether he or she is already on staff or brought in from the outside. Build a comprehensive, end-to-end plan that defines the **portfolio** of projects required to execute the Steering Committee's priorities. The Program Management Plan (PMP) should include a formal charter for *each* project, with stakeholder agreement on project scope, objectives, key timelines, resources, and defined success criteria. Use a Work Breakdown Structure (WBS) to decompose each project into smaller components in terms of size, duration and responsibility. Define and group the discrete work elements in a way that makes the most sense for your particular organization. Use the WBS for your detailed cost estimating, controls and deliverables. Set realistic, achievable milestones.

The Program Management Plan defined in the paragraph above is not to be confused with the project manager or the project management plans he or she may create. The Program Management Plan described here is a comprehensive portfolio of all projects across the enterprise that contribute – in one way or another – to the ultimate success of the ITSM improvement initiative. Just as an investment portfolio may consist of many different types of investments, the enterprise Program Management Plan may consist of many discrete and different projects.

Note: Every milestone defined in the various project plans that contribute to the Program Management Plan (PMP) should have at least one deliverable associated with it. Scrutinize the project plan(s) and rigorously question any milestone that lacks a firm deliverable. Chances are, it's an artificial milestone, and can be eliminated.

Project management design principles, such as the 100% rule, mutually exclusive elements, level of detail and coding scheme will not be covered in this work. We assume that these design principles are routinely used when generating project plans within one's respective organization. Readers unfamiliar with project management practices are encouraged to research the wealth of material on this topic that is published and maintained by the Project Management Institute.[12]

Anyone who has managed a large Program can attest to the excruciating level of detail required to plan and coordinate the many activities, tasks and resources involved in executing a major strategic initiative. The prospect of soliciting stakeholder input and gaining stakeholder approval for such detailed plans can be even more daunting. For these reasons, we strongly advocate creating a high-level graphical roadmap as a tool for *communicating*, and *soliciting*, information from key stakeholders.

The ITSM Transformation Roadmap provides a "snapshot" of all planned implementation and improvement activities over the Program lifecycle. *Figure 12* shows a sample roadmap format built using Microsoft® Excel®. Many consulting companies have developed proprietary roadmap tools, and your organization may have a preferred format – if so, we encourage you to use it. What is important is not the format, but that the roadmap contains the vital information needed to communicate and gain buy-in from stakeholders, including:

- The key IT capabilities to be developed, logically grouped and prioritized.
- The Business- and IT strategy-driven milestones our activities must align to.

---

12 *http://www.pmi.org*.

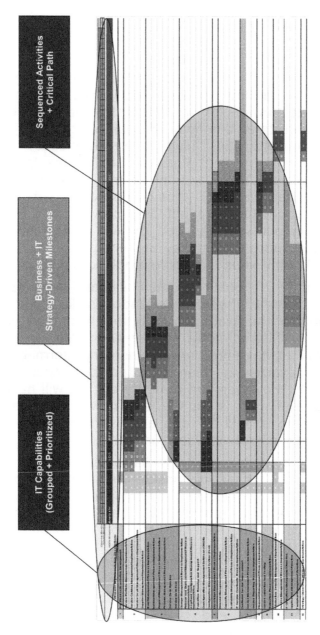

Figure 12: ITSM Transformation Roadmap

As the Roadmap is developed, continually validate assumptions and priorities with all key stakeholders, including senior leadership, the ITSM Steering Committee, and process and service owners (to the extent these roles exist in your organization). Proactively address disagreements on priorities or activity sequencing. One of Michael Dell's enduring philosophies is that one should learn to love bad news – to seek it out! It is *much* easier to resolve conflicts at this level of analysis, than to wait until detailed project plans have been developed. Reaching agreement on the final Roadmap may take longer than expected, and, at times, may seem like an unnecessary, over-politicized exercise – but do not lose heart! The ITSM Transformation Roadmap not only provides the foundation for building out your detailed project plans, but cements buy-in and support from key stakeholders, which you can draw upon later when inevitable roadblocks pop up.

This roadmap should be the billboard advertising the activities to come. If your organization is like many we have seen, much of the strategy activity that has taken place thus far has not filtered down to the line staff. Specific staff members may have received rudimentary information; some staff may even have been assigned to temporarily assist your efforts. However, the majority of staff will have only a vague idea of what is coming, and how it will affect them. The roadmap should be one arrow among many in your communications quiver. Use it unhesitatingly.

Have staff make copies, and display it in every common area you can think of: inside elevators (if practical), bathroom stall doors(!), the company cafeteria, break rooms, conference rooms, etc. Carry a copy to every meeting you attend, and refer to it often. Collar passers-by and use it as a conversation starter, or use it to provide impromptu updates to folks who may be tangentially involved. Make sure everyone knows that the ITSM implementation effort is moving from the strategy stage into the design stage, and that development activities are scheduled to begin. The roadmap proves that the organization is moving along, and that progress is being made.

By giving the roadmap this type of visibility, you are sending a clear, unambiguous message that executive leadership and line management are serious about bringing an IT service management culture and mindset into the organization. It will send the message to the staff that this effort is real, is supported in full by leadership, and that it deserves nothing less than their full attention and commitment.

In summary, the actions you want to take in this step are:

1. Negotiate the order in which prioritized capabilities will be developed.

2. Achieve an optimal outcome for your ITSM Transformation by advising on trade-offs and emphasizing shared services, infrastructure and processes.

3. Issue a Notice of Decision when negotiations are complete.

4. Produce an IT Strategic Plan that addresses how IT will build, operate and sustain the capabilities required to deliver customer requirements.

5. Build a Goal Linking matrix.

6. Develop a Program Management Plan that defines the portfolio of projects required to execute the ITSM Steering Committee's priorities.

7. Generate and publish the ITSM Transformation Roadmap to project staff and all relevant stakeholders, as well as to the Business Sponsor.

8. Construct, approve and publish tactical project plans.

CHAPTER 7: DEFINE ORGANIZATIONAL ROLES AND RESPONSIBILITIES

Prior to commencing with **Step Seven**, let's review what has been produced through the first six stages of the Ten-Step approach.

In hand, we have the following deliverables:

1. A completed and approved Business Plan.
2. Initial funding to cover preliminary activities.
3. A comprehensive current-state assessment, including service costs and resource allocations.
4. A defined service portfolio, including identification of key gaps and prioritized future investments.
5. An established governing body, tasked with overseeing and guiding the ITSM Transformation.
6. An approved, agreed-upon ideal target state.
7. A rank-ordered list of prioritized capabilities.
8. An IT strategic plan aligned with business initiatives.
9. An ITSM Program Management Plan and Transformation Roadmap to guide tactical execution.

Most organizations – at this point – would green-light moving forward, and immediately commence service and process design. A point of fact: a recent client did exactly that with less than stellar results. Due to a lack of clarity regarding who was responsible for what activity at the varying points in the process, the client ended up spending more money than anticipated, and, at the end of the exercise, had virtually nothing to show for their efforts, other than a great deal of shelf-ware documentation.

Why did this happen? Simply put, the primary reason was the failure to establish a standardized set of enterprise roles and responsibilities, both to govern and to manage ITSM development.

> **Note:** *governance* and *management* are not the same,[13] these functions are almost always performed by different roles!

COBIT® practitioners – familiar with the Align, Plan and Organize (APO) domain – understand that a critical component in creating an effective IT organization is the establishment of standardized roles and responsibilities. Likewise, establishing standardized roles to govern and manage service management activities is a key requirement set forth in the ISO/IEC 20000 standard. We could cite other frameworks and standards as well, but the bottom line is this: *do not* commence development without *first* defining key roles, and then assigning those roles to competent, qualified individuals in your organization.

Having fulfilled the critical necessity of defining key roles and responsibilities, the question is, "Where does one start?" The ITIL® publications make reference to nearly 100 service management roles, and this is by no means an exhaustive list. In fact, there are entire frameworks developed specifically to address roles and resource management in IT. One framework we have encountered in our client work is the Skills Framework for the Information Age® (SFIA), which places an emphasis on skills identification and development.

---

13 See the updated COBIT® standard (version 5) available at *http://www.isaca.org/COBIT/Pages/default.aspx* for an excellent treatment of governance vs. management functions.

Unfortunately, a complete discussion of service management roles would make this volume too unwieldy to read and use; however, two points are worth making here. First, not all roles are created equal – focus on **first principles**. In every organization for which we have provided consulting, the roles of *process owner* and *service owner* have proven *absolutely critical* to ITSM success. Organizations may call these by different names (e.g. "process lead," "product manager," etc.) and the roles' scope of authority and responsibilities may vary somewhat. Nevertheless, always ensure there is a single accountable individual (e.g. a belly button to poke, a throat to choke) for *every* process and service in your organization. This is especially important if you are developing a new capability, or launching a targeted improvement initiative.

While we don't normally recommend the practice in larger and more mature organizations, it is technically acceptable for an individual to wear multiple hats. This is especially true for processes or services that are tightly coupled. For example, you may assign a single individual as the process owner for both availability and capacity management, or a single service owner to steward all telecommunication services. The most important thing is that *someone in your organization* is truly accountable for the *end-to-end performance* of the process or service, and that this responsibility cannot be delegated away. End-to-end operation comprises all aspects of process or service performance, including its metrics (CSFs, KPIs, continual improvement goals, etc.)

The second point is this: role creation and assignment shouldn't be confined to IT – it must be a joint effort with the business. If the organization intends to be truly effective – if it is serious about adopting a Service Management culture and mindset across the enterprise – then standardized enterprise roles are mandatory. Not only must every process have a clearly defined process owner, but process owners must work together to ensure that enterprise processes are designed to be standardized, repeatable, and interoperable across all domains of the organization. The same logic applies to service ownership as well, particularly in the case of enterprise "shared services."

Likewise, the IT department should not be the stewards of services and capabilities. We have participated in many rousing arguments over the question of whether enterprise processes like change management are owned by IT or the business. In this matter, we reserve judgment. However, IT should *never* own services or capabilities. IT is responsible for *service delivery*, but ownership responsibilities belong to the business, and it is the business that must drive and guide IT's efforts. Without business involvement, the Service Management effort will fail.

RACI chart and variations

Now that we have established a basic understanding of *what* we need to do to establish roles and responsibilities (and its importance to our ITSM success), it's time to address *how* to do it. Here, we see so no need to reinvent a well-greased wheel. The clear tool of choice, as suggested in the ITIL® publications, is the RACI chart. We will begin by briefly reviewing the RACI concept and its variations; however, our primary objective is to share some of our hard-won experience on how to go about corralling the right people and actually building out a top-level enterprise RACI.

For those unfamiliar with the acronym, RACI stands for **R**esponsible, **A**ccountable, **C**onsulted, and **I**nformed. For each activity and task, it defines the individual or group that must be involved with a given activity or task.

Accountable: The individual – and, in our opinion, it must be an individual – deemed **a**ccountable is the person at whom "the buck stops." For each activity or task, there can be one – and only one – accountable individual. Otherwise, there can be no accountability. Typically, this is the individual directing and orchestrating everything that must happen within the given activity or task.

Responsible: The individual or group that is deemed responsible is the person doing the actual work. He (or the department, if that is the case) is the entity executing the activity's procedures and generating required deliverables. An activity or task may have more than one responsible individual assigned. Regardless of how many responsible parties are assigned, the responsible role receives direction from the person who is accountable, even if he, she or they don't directly report to him or her.

Consulted: People, or departments, that must be consulted are typically those who influence, or are influenced by, the activity or task in question. Individuals who are consulted are those who usually provide data and information to the activity or task in question, or who are dependent upon the output of the activity or task. They may also be subject matter experts (SMEs) possessing specialized knowledge or skills that are essential to the activity or task's execution. In certain cases, the person who must be consulted may be a person in the organization whose input is crucial to a pending decision. In all cases, two-way communication is assumed and understood. For some activities or tasks, execution cannot be completed without this person's involvement.

Informed: Individuals or departments that must be informed are those who will typically be affected by the activity or task, but whose input is not *required*. One-way communication – usually from the accountable individual – is assumed and understood.

There are many variations of the standard RACI chart. Project Management aficionados often use the RASCI model, where "S" denotes support resources allocated to the *responsible* individual. Financial organizations sometimes use the "S" designation to indicate that a person must have "Sign-off" for the activity or task. In our opinion, if a person "signs-off" on an activity, then that person is (and should be) deemed *accountable*.

RACI-VS charts are popular within the manufacturing and software development communities. Here, the *Verifier* (the individual who checks whether the product meets the acceptance criteria set forth in the product description) and *Signatory* (the individual(s) that approve the verify decision and authorize the product hand-off) roles are added to the standard RACI matrix.

Another variation that is gaining popularity is RACIO (or, alternatively, CAIRO) which adds the "Out of the Loop" designation to the standard RACI chart. In our view, dysfunctional organizations are the ones that are most fond of this RACI model, and we hope this usage isn't endemic to your organization.

If at all possible, avoid the variations. In our estimation, variations cause more confusion than clarification, and add an undesirable level of bureaucracy to the process. The simpler the RACI chart, the easier it will be for people to understand, accept and use it.

The RACI chart is an invaluable tool for clearly laying out who needs to be involved for each activity and task, and for specifying that person's level of involvement. It places accountability directly where it belongs, and helps ensure that the right people are involved at critical junctures, and in rendering key decisions.

It goes without saying that high-level activities across the enterprise must first be defined before any RACI exercise can take place. We will pull this thread a little more firmly as this discussion progresses, but it's important that the organization at least agree upon the high-level activities necessary for service management success.

Experience has shown that mandatory off-site sessions are the best way to build these RACI charts. At this point in your Transformation journey, you should have little difficulty convincing executive management to schedule this. Without exception, every company we have worked with has recognized the value of setting aside a day or two to lay out a high-level plan. Make sure to extend the invitation to your strategic suppliers, as well as to your senior executives and business unit leaders. These business partners have a critical role to play in the firm's success or failure. Involving them at the outset ensures they not only understand the objective, but are committed to its success. However, be sure to utilize "closed-door" sessions to discuss sensitive or politically charged topics.

Before convening the session, convince the sponsor (ideally the CEO, Agency Director, etc.) to issue this one simple rule: invitees who choose not to attend, or who fail to send a qualified proxy to participate on their behalf, do not, afterwards, get a voice or an opportunity to change or influence a previously taken vote. It is imperative that all attendees have confidence that decisions agreed to at the offsite will be upheld and enforced; retroactive non-concurrence or vetoes after the fact are *verboten*.

The agenda is straightforward. Attendees are there to decide who will do what, and when those people will do them. That last statement bears repeating. It is imperative that everyone knows, understands, and agrees upon the activities that must be accomplished, and the persons who will be responsible for executing them. For each activity, identify the person who will be ultimately accountable; the person who is responsible for doing the actual work; the people who must be consulted; and the people who must be informed.

As part of this assignment, agree upon the time-frame in which the activity or task must be completed. Ascertain whether the required input has a dependency or constraint that must be taken into account. Specify how those inputs will be delivered (e.g. via an electronic data feed, a hard-copy report, an instant message notification, etc.) Conduct the same exercise for any produced outputs. Make this a strategic negotiation, and **not** a technical exercise. Participants have to buy into the process in order for it to work. Therefore, be careful not to dictate based on preconceived notions of how things *should* run. As the group works through the exercise, they will gradually come to a consensus based on practical and political considerations.

One of the "do not do this" examples we want to include here is the mistake of assigning Process and Service Ownership based upon the principle of "this person is available." The act of naming Process and Service Ownership should be viewed as seriously as appointing a Chief Financial Officer. The Service Owner, for example, will be accountable for the delivery and support of a major service offering. They must be trained, knowledgeable, competent, and capable of carrying out the duties and responsibilities inherent in the job.

The same is true of Process Owners. The owner of the Service Asset and Configuration Management (SACM) process – to provide just one example – must be grounded in the practical implications of establishing functional, allocated, and technical baselines, and the importance of keeping them accurate and up-to-date. Too many other processes depend on SACM to assign it to someone who has no experience or little understanding of the process's intricacies.

Service and Process Owners steward the firm's offered services and the underlying processes supporting the delivery of those services. It is their joint duty to ensure that service offerings meet the client's current and evolving needs. Service owners are the "face" of the organization to its customers, and, as such, will have the greatest amount of input into future service design and delivery discussions. Without clearly assigned ownership, there is the very real possibility that services will fail to live up to customer expectations. When that happens, customers typically move on to service providers who can and will satisfy their expectations.

Figure 13: Enterprise RACI Chart

	Board of Directors	Executive Committee	CIO	ITSM Steering Committee	Architecture Review Board	Change Advisory Board	Service Owner Council	Service Owner	Business Relationship Manager	Process Owner Council	Process Owner	Process Manager	Strategic Business Unit-1	Strategic Business Unit-2	Strategic Business Unit-3	etc...
KEY: R = Responsible A = Accountable C = Consulted I = Informed																
Services																
1.0 Activity ABC…																
2.0 Activity XYZ…																
Processes																
3.0 Activity ABC…																
4.0 Activity XYZ…																
Capabilities																
5.0 Activity ABC…																
6.0 Activity XYZ…																

ENTERPRISE

This step is the firm's opportunity to consider (if required) additional requirements for staff, skills, functions, authority, accountability, roles and responsibilities, and supervision. Conducting this exercise provides transparency and control, as well as ensuring the involvement of senior executives, key business managers and strategic suppliers. Once this exercise has been completed, the ITSM Steering Committee can (if applicable) adjust and prioritize IT resources in line with business needs. *Figure 13* is an example of an enterprise RACI chart.

This example is demonstrative of the broad scope and vast organizational impact of your ITSM Transformation effort. Note that the exercise begins with assessing accountability at the very top levels of the organization – the Board of Directors, Executive Committee, C-level Executives, etc. We cannot tell you how many times we have asked to view an IT organization's RACI chart, only to be shown an activity or task-level RACI for the incident management process, listing the process manager as the highest authority. This point must be clearly understood: *process RACI charts are not enough!* And, furthermore, they are the wrong place to start. Process RACIs, while vitally important, should only be developed after higher-level governance has been agreed upon and put in place. "Bottoms up" governance never works; governance must always be established at the top and promulgated down.

Continuing to the right in *Figure 13*, the next several columns show examples of higher-level governance bodies, councils or committees that may play a service management role in your organization. Depending on your organization's enterprise governance model (or lack thereof), your organization may have only one key body that plays a role in service management activities (such as a Service Management Office). For most organizations, there will be many, e.g. the architecture board, change board, configuration board, project management office, risk board, etc. It should be noted here that assigning functional roles to boards, committees, or even entire departments is okay if the glove fits; however, be sure to clearly articulate to everyone that the "buck stops" with one – *and only one* – named individual, e.g. the Committee Chair, Department Head, etc.

Continuing further to the right, we have provided examples of key service and process ownership roles that should be considered. As mentioned previously, these roles are particularly important in both the tactical execution and long-term success of the ITSM initiative. The assignment of these roles depends heavily on the culture, size, and ITSM maturity of your organization. Ownership "Councils," for example, are typically found in larger, mature enterprises with multiple business units. Some smaller organizations combine the roles of Process Owner and Process Manager under one person – a practice we advise that you avoid, if it is at all possible. The primary rationale for this suggestion is that the normal separation of duties (strategic vision and mission versus the day-to-day operational responsibilities) often becomes blurred, and, in some instances, completely eradicated. The old adage of *"when you are up to your waist in alligators, it's hard to remember your original intention was to drain the swamp"* applies here in spades.

Finally, the last few columns highlight the importance of assigning accountability and responsibility to the business units that are both the *owners* and *customers* of ITSM. There are, of course, many other possibilities to consider – the RACI chart will always be a unique reflection of your individual organization.

The most basic approach to a "top-level" organizational RACI is one where role designations are applied not to a single process or service, but to *all* processes and services. For example, when completed, this chart would show what the Change Advisory Board (CAB) is accountable and responsible for, and where it must be consulted and informed, in respect to any process or service. This level of analysis can be a good way to catalyze the initial conversation, or be used as a fallback technique to reboot conversations that have stalled.

However, there will of course be processes and/or services where the CAB may play a greater or lesser role, or may only be involved in one particular activity or phase of the lifecycle. For this reason, we typically recommend (based on the size of the organization and the scope of its ITSM Program) taking the level of analysis one level deeper. For processes, this means assigning **R**s, **A**s, **C**s and **I**s not only to the top-level process, but also to each of its high-level activities. If a process is new for your organization, use the high-level activities defined in the ITIL® framework. These are based on universal good practice and will likely be similar in your environment. Most meaningful process tailoring occurs at the sub-activity, task, and work instruction levels. For services, we recommend using the lifecycle phases (e.g. strategy, design, transition, operation, continual improvement) as the next level of role attribution.

Do not – we repeat – *do not* attempt to define roles and responsibilities beyond the level of detail described in the previous paragraph. Detailed activity and task-level RACIs will be produced as part of detailed design, which is discussed in the next chapter. Any effort to accomplish this level of detail now is a waste of time, and risks creating ill will and setting back the entire effort. Establishing an agreed and leadership-approved enterprise RACI that is aligned with the organization's enterprise governance model is a major step forward in your ITSM journey – don't overshoot! The top-level enterprise RACI will become the all-important "Rosetta Stone" that design teams will use to ensure all lower-level RACIs align to each other, and collectively support the achievement of your ITSM Transformation goals.

Organizational change management

Before moving on to the next phase of the ITSM Transformation initiative, we would like to take a moment to touch upon the topic of organizational change management. We have mentioned several times before that this improvement initiative will fundamentally alter the organization's culture and dynamics. In the studied opinion of numerous experts in the field, the people aspect of any ITSM improvement initiative is the most critical. Several books have been written on the subject, but the most prominent and widely known is *Leading Change*, Harvard Business Press (1996), written by Dr John Kotter.

Dr Kotter champions an eight-stage process. *Figure 14* is a graphical representation of Dr Kotter's principles. For now, we will address the first six stages, as these are the most relevant to our discussion. The final two stages (Consolidating Gains and Producing More Change, and Anchoring New Approaches in the Culture), are incorporated into Step 10 of the Ten-Step approach, where we discuss the Balanced Scorecard and Continual Improvement.

Figure 14: Eight-stage process of creating major change

Establishing a sense of urgency
- Examining the market and competitive realities
- Identifying and discussing crises, potential crises, or major opportunities.

Creating the guiding coalition
- Putting together a group with enough power to lead the change
- Getting the group to work together like a team.

Developing a Vision and Strategy
- Creating a vision to help direct the change effort
- Developing strategies for achieving that vision.

Communicating the Change Vision
- Using every vehicle possible to constantly communicate the new vision and strategies
- Having the guiding coalition mode the behavior expected of employees.

Empowering broad-based action
- Getting rid of obstacles
- Changing systems or structures that undermine the change vision
- Encouraging risk-taking and nontraditional ideas, activities and actions.

Generating short-term wins
- Planning for visible improvements in performance, or "wins"
- Creating those wins
- Visibly recognizing and rewarding people who made wins possible.

Consolidating gains and producing more change
- Using increased credibility to change all systems, structures and policies that don't fit together and fit the transformation vision
- Hiring, promoting and developing people who can implement the change vision
- Reinvigorating the process with new projects, themes, and change agents.

Anchoring new approaches in the culture
- Creating better performance through customer- and productivity-oriented behavior, more and better leadership, and more effective management
- Articulating the connections between new behaviors and organizational success
- Developing means to ensure leadership development and succession.

Let's assess how well our efforts have thus far aligned to Dr Kotter's Principles.

1: Establishing a Sense of Urgency: We can successfully argue that the sense of urgency was created by the Board of Directors when they articulated their vision and set out the goals they wanted the organization to achieve.

2: Creating the Guiding Coalition: By establishing the ITSM Steering Committee, comprised of key business leaders throughout the organization, we have created a coalition designed to guide and shepherd the service management improvement initiative through its full lifecycle. When and where necessary, additional guiding coalitions may be spun up to oversee or execute short-term tactical objectives.

3: Developing a Vision and Strategy Vision: The negotiation and creation of the IT Ecosystem developed a graphic representation of the new model that will be designed and built. This change vision is not only the primary communication device for executives and staff – it is also the overarching blueprint for the organization's future model.

4: Communicating the Change Vision: Involving all key business leaders in the creation of the IT Ecosystem was the vehicle used for communicating the vision and obtaining staff acceptance and buy-in. Every relevant stakeholder had the opportunity to review and contribute to the model's creation. The ITSM Transformation Roadmap also serves as a powerful tool for communicating how the organization will jointly execute the vision.

5: Empowering Broad-based Action: By virtue of its creation and charter, the ITSM Steering Committee was granted the authority to take broad-based action for the improvement initiatives being considered. It is charged with removing the obstacles to change, has the authority to change systems or structures that seriously undermine the vision, and can take acceptable risks that fall within the parameters established by the enterprise Risk Management Board.

6: Generating Short-Term Wins: Thus far, several short-term wins (an approved Business Plan; the IT Infrastructure and Costs spreadsheet; a chartered ITSM Steering Committee) have already been achieved. Touting these achievements is necessary to let the naysayers and fence-sitters know that genuine progress is being made.

7: Consolidating Gains and Producing More Change: Methods for achieving this are discussed at length in *Chapter 15*, which deals with Continual Improvement.

8: Anchoring New Approaches in the Culture: Your improvement initiative will only succeed if more effective and better leadership and governance is continually applied. *Chapter 15*, dealing with the use of the Balanced Scorecard and Continual Improvement, will suggest a variety of ways in which to "bake in" the new approaches into your organizational culture.

With this assessment, it can be fairly argued that our ITSM improvement initiative is well on its way to successfully achieving the organization's broad goals and objectives, and that we are actively considering the organizational change management aspects of our project.

If you are unfamiliar with Dr Kotter's seminal work, or if it has been a few years since you've last reviewed it, take the time to familiarize yourself with Dr Kotter's Principles. In one of our client engagements, we also found Dr Kotter's subsequent book, *Our Iceberg is Melting,* Kotter J and Rathgeber H, St. Martin's Press (2006), to be a highly effective and practical means to quickly educate (and inspire!) key stakeholders on the radical change process they were about to embark upon. This short, 160-page book provides the clearest description we have seen of the importance of identifying and enlisting "change champions," winning over the "fence-sitters," and marginalizing "change resisters."

Without a clear understanding of the pitfalls and potential obstacles you may face (and a cohesive strategy for dealing with them), your organization will join the long, sad list of many that have tried, and failed, to implement a Service Management Model. The 32nd President of the United States, Franklin Delano Roosevelt, once remarked that the thing he feared most was trying to lead, only to turn around and find no one following. Don't let this happen to you. Anticipate, plan for, and remediate the people problems **before** they happen. You and your organization will be better served for it.

With that said, we are now ready to put processes, administrative policies, and procedures in place for all capabilities and functions, with specific attention to standardization, control, quality assurance, risk management, security, and data ownership.

In summary, the actions you want to take in this step are:

1. Assess staff skills, functions, authority, accountability, roles, responsibilities and required level of supervision.
2. Schedule executive off-site session(s) with clearly established and enforced "rules of the game."
3. Build out a top-level enterprise RACI that aligns to enterprise governance.
4. Validate and continue Organizational Change Management activities.

CHAPTER 8: STANDARDIZED DEVELOPMENT APPROACH

For those readers who have journeyed with us through the previous Seven Steps, we offer hearty congratulations! You should be proud of what you have accomplished thus far! We also recognize that some readers reside in organizations where the foundational building blocks have already been erected; so whether you skimmed through Steps One to Seven as a refresher, or skipped straight to Step Eight, we welcome you to this decisive point in the Transformation journey.

Regardless of how you got here, there is *good news* to be had. In many ways, the biggest obstacles (and risks) to ITSM success are behind you. Let's quickly review what has been accomplished. In Steps One to Four, you addressed the service strategy phase of the lifecycle by documenting enterprise objectives, analyzing service financials, understanding and documenting current and future service demand, and chartering a service portfolio overseen by a representative governance body. As you entered the Service Design phase in Steps Five to Seven, you completed a high-level design by defining a target state service management ecosystem, negotiating development priorities, creating an execution plan and roadmap, and forging agreement on roles and responsibilities.

It is important to understand what has been accomplished (or, for the lucky few, what was already in place) because these service strategy and high-level design artifacts provide the foundation for everything that comes next: detailed design, transition, operations, and last, but not least, continual improvement.

Step Eight marks the beginning of detailed design. While this may come as a welcome relief to those of you more attuned to granular-level details than high-level strategy, you must also understand that complete coverage of this topic would require its own publication. In fact, it is interesting to note that the latest version of ITIL® addresses design in much greater detail than in previous versions, going so far as to add dedicated design roles and even elevating design as its *own process* in the framework.

Given this context, in Step Eight we will focus on the traditional ITSM discipline of *process design* to demonstrate how a structured enterprise approach to development helps us achieve the critical goals of standardized, repeatable and interoperable enterprise processes. In reality, each IT capability, function, service, process, etc. must go through its own mini-lifecycle of planning, design, development, transition, operation and improvement. While we recognize there are significant differences in the approach taken to designing, say, a service versus a process, we feel the lessons drawn from standardizing process design can be applied to the design of other ITSM elements.

Note: Due to the complexity of Steps Eight through Ten of our approach, we have elected to address the various components over the course of the next several chapters.

There are many reasons to advocate using a standardized approach to process development. Above all, standardization is essential to achieving both efficiency and effectiveness. As the economist Ronald Coase demonstrated in his influential work *The Nature of the Firm, Economica,* 4:16 (1937), 386-405 [14] the very existence of a firm or organization is evidence of the desire to produce maximum results with minimum required resources. All organizations seek to be more efficient and effective, regardless of mission – this is equally true of commercial-/profit-maximizing firms, government agencies, non-profit organizations, or any

---

14 http://en.wikipedia.org/wiki/The_Nature_of_the_Firm.

variation of an organization thereof. Of course, achieving this state of nirvana is anything but assured – this is why the role of service management is so critical to an organization's success.

In addition, there are many second-order effects of standardization that include, but are not limited to, the following. A standard approach:

- Provides general direction and guidance for employees: a solid, yet flexible, framework within which to operate.
- Improves communication within and between teams and, therefore, lessens the possibility of confusion and misaligned expectations.
- Greatly reduces the learning curve and training time for new or retrained employees.
- Enriches the consistency of the work effort across the enterprise.
- Ensures business continuity, and aids in quickly recovering from natural or man-made disasters.
- Allows for easier and more efficient delegation of routine tasks to lower-level employees.

To summarize, achieving process repeatability is the Holy Grail of service management. It virtually guarantees that the organization can rapidly scale (either up or down) to meet customer demand. Delivering the right amount of service with the necessary number of resources maximizes the bottom line, and promotes the overall health and well-being of the organization.

The underlying question is, and always has been: where and how should the line be drawn between enterprise-wide standards, and those standards that may be required for departmental- or geographical-specific requirements?

To satisfy customer demand, every organization must strike the optimal balance between enterprise standardization and the need to tailor individual processes to fit the unique needs of a particular business unit or wholly-owned subsidiary. A prime example of this is an international organization having branch offices in several different countries. Local rules and regulations may necessitate an exception or modification to an enterprise standard. Failure to do so may subject the organization to fines or penalties. It therefore behooves the enterprise to allow the local entity to modify existing standards, while continuing to adhere – as closely as possible – to enterprise policies, procedures and standards. This is important because enterprise efficiency and effectiveness can only be achieved through some degree of standardization. However, both measures ultimately suffer if standards are so rigid that individual business units are not able to apply the principles of a process to meet the unique needs of its customer base, or to adequately support a delivered service. Without flexibility and the authority to innovate, the business unit will inevitably resort to costly and inefficient workarounds, or, worse, will establish their own standards that may be at odds with inter-dependent processes and business controls.

The CIO is responsible for developing and enforcing a standard process framework for the enterprise. He or she should use the IT strategic plan and a tailored combination of industry best-practice frameworks to best meet the organization's needs. When completed, it should consist of a complete set of processes, controls and metrics that support the current and future IT Service Portfolio. Using this organization-specific framework as a baseline, process design teams are then allowed the freedom to tailor lower-level process activities, tasks, work instructions and tool functionality to fit the individual customer needs, budget and operational constraints of each business unit.

For example, there must be one – **and only one** – enterprise process for accepting, evaluating, approving, coordinating, and closing a change, i.e. an Enterprise

Change Management process. However, within each of these standard, high-level process activities, each business unit may tailor how a request for change is created and by whom, who within the business unit has the authority to review and approve it for submission, the degree to which the business unit utilizes enterprise tools and/or proprietary tools internal to its process, and the business-specific evaluation criteria and prioritization assigned to the change.

Figure 15 is a graphical representation of the four levels of process development, culminating with the integration of people, process and tools to make the process operational. On the left-hand side, the figure emphasizes the balancing act between CIO-sponsored enterprise standards (Levels I and II) and the inherent need for business unit flexibility to tailor process designs to meet their own unique customer and operational needs (Levels III and IV).

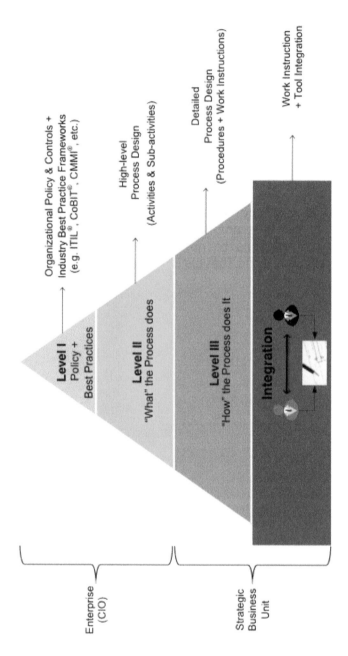

Figure 15: ITSM process development pyramid

This method and model may not be suitable for your organization, but, in situations where it is, you – as the ITSM practitioner – must work to find that optimal balance.

You may encounter resistance when first advocating that business units be granted this degree of latitude. Centralized authorities are typically reluctant to issue exceptions or modifications because they see it as the first step to total anarchy. In fact, anecdotal evidence points to the contrary. Remote branches and business units are more likely to adhere to enterprise standards when given the leeway to modify the standards to accommodate local conditions. If you encounter this situation in your organization, use the process development pyramid to foster dialogue with all relevant parties.

Figure 15 aligns to the ISO/IEC 20000 standard. It breaks the development approach into four primary categories:

1. Policy and best practices
2. High-level Process Design
3. Detailed Process Design
4. Work Instructions and Tool Integration.

The first tier

The first tier specifies – at the enterprise level – organizational policies, risk appetite, quality standards, adherence to regulatory directives, and any desired management controls the organization wishes to put into place. It mandates the parameters within which lower-level business units or subsidiary companies will operate. Although rare, some executives – perhaps unduly influenced by a consultant with a particular area of expertise to sell – will try to dictate which of the industry best-practice frameworks are used. One firm was so insistent on the use of Lean Six Sigma that its use was a major factor determining each line manager's annual compensation. While you cannot ignore such organizational realities, the smart practitioner will fight for the right to use *any* tool that best fits the task at hand; in reality, this often involves combining elements from multiple frameworks.

One notable exception is where there exists an organizational mandate for ISO/IEC 20000 compliance. As an ITSM expert, you can advise the organization's leadership on the merits and drawbacks (usually the cost) of pursuing or maintaining ISO certification. Achieving certification *can* be a big feather in your cap, and, if the organization can capture sufficient value from the investment, your ITSM Transformation initiative is the perfect vehicle for doing it. However, this is ultimately an executive decision that must be made in consideration of many factors – for example, whether or not the organization is already ISO9000 certified (or wishes to be). If certifying compliance is part of your ITSM mandate, then the ISO/IEC standard must be paramount; however, do keep in mind that ISO/IEC 20000 is designed to be compatible and synergistic with other frameworks – most notably ITIL®, but also CMMI®, COBIT®, Six Sigma, etc.

While on the subject of international standards, it should be noted that *other* ISO/IEC standards may need to be taken into account when designing your development framework. ISO/IEC 27001 (information security), ISO/IEC 38500 (IT governance), and ISO/IEC 15504 (process assessment) are three examples of prominent standards that can be factored into your development approach, with or without a mandate for ISO/IEC 20000 certification.

The second tier

The second tier of the pyramid describes **what** each service and process will do – not *how* it will be done.

Let's use Amazon.com as an example of how this might work in the retail environment. Amazon's CEO may direct that one of the company's offered services be the sale and delivery of books to potential customers. (In this example, we will limit our attention to printed books. E-books will have their own unique set of activities and tasks.) Once the CEO has approved and funded this particular goal, his involvement in establishing this line of business is essentially finished. It is now up to the Service Owner (and the supporting Process Owners and line managers) to define the tactical and procedural steps necessary to meet the requirements the CEO has set out.

The third tier

The tactical and procedural steps are defined in the pyramid's third tier. It is here that the required detailed activities and tasks are spelled out. Taking the example cited in the paragraph above a step further, the Service Owner, tasked with achieving the CEO's mandate of offering and delivering books to customers, would outline the broad activities necessary to accomplish the goal (e.g. negotiate an arrangement with one or more publishers, design a web-based application displaying the products for sale, engage the marketing and advertising department to publicize the service offering, etc.) In project management terms, this is the beginning of the Work Breakdown Structure (WBS), which should comprise the components of the project plan directing these activities.

Once the broad activities had been defined, the Service Owner would then necessarily turn his or her attention to the various tasks comprising each defined activity. In the case of negotiating an arrangement with one or more publishers, the Service Owner would perform (or delegate) the following tasks:

- Identify the publisher's point of contact.
- Arrange a meeting.
- Specify desired outcomes.

- Discuss logistical considerations (e.g. distribution/delivery channels).
- Reach an agreement on costs/fees/revenue sharing.
- Draw up the contract.
- Execute the contract.

Note: The tasks listed above are for illustrative purposes only, and are not meant to be exhaustive or comprehensive.

The Service Owner (or designee) would perform a similar exercise for each additional activity, until all tasks have been identified.

The fourth tier

The pyramid's fourth tier – the foundational level – is where identified tasks are further decomposed into work instructions: the step-by-step procedures spelling out how operations or administrative staff will perform their day-to-day responsibilities. The work instruction documents the use of supporting tools, and should – if properly written – include tips and techniques for initial troubleshooting and incident resolution. This level of detail invests the operator with the maximum amount of authority and autonomy allowed them by senior management.

Execution: Integrated Process Development Teams

As any experienced practitioner or consultant will tell you, much of your ITSM success (or lack thereof) ultimately comes down to *execution*. Flawless execution by a high-performance team of experts can make even a mediocre plan look brilliant in hindsight; likewise, poor or uncoordinated execution can quickly render the best-laid plans useless.

8: Standardized Development Approach

At the end of this chapter, we describe a standardized process development methodology (PDLC) that has worked well for us in multiple client engagements. *Chapters 9-14* further lay out the details of each phase. You may opt to tailor this approach to fit your organizational environment, or you may choose to use a different approach entirely. In your role as "ITSM General," the development methodology serves as your battle plan. It is your tactical, step-by-step guide to achieving the desired result of standardized, repeatable and interoperable enterprise processes.

But, as any general knows, a battle plan – while essential – is often not enough. A general can only oversee activities; he or she cannot engage in every battle. As the ITSM General, you'll require trusted commanders who can quickly adjust to changing battlefield conditions. Forces skilled at conducting battle by land, air, and sea must be at your disposal. You'll require intelligence and tactical weapons experts, and, most importantly, in order to ensure an adequate supply of personnel and munitions, you'll need a secure and reliable supply chain. Above all, you'll need a command and control center to monitor conditions on the ground – one that provides you with real-time data and intelligence for rendering required decisions. All of these disparate "force elements" must be trained to understand their roles, and act as an integrated fighting force.

While we realize the battlefield analogy may seem a bit extreme, we have also seen the failure to adopt a solid process development methodology "kill" many ITSM initiatives dead in its tracks. We've witnessed this first-hand, and have no desire to see your organization suffer the same fate. Process development is arduous, it is costly, and it is inherently political. Imagine being in the heat of a battle, ready to charge and take a hill, only to turn around and find that your key allies have defected to the other side. Sadly, we have seen this happen, as well. Process development not only requires significant investment in time, money and organizational resources, but, at the end of the day, it dictates how people do their jobs and how power (however you define it) is distributed throughout the enterprise.

For all of these reasons, we highly recommend taking the time to think through how to best structure and staff your process development effort. A seasoned general doesn't develop a battle plan overnight – and neither should you. After much trial and error, we have found that an integrated team approach, with strong coordination and oversight from a central authority, works best. This is especially true in larger enterprises with multiple independent business units. *Figure 16*, below, depicts what an integrated process development team structure might look like for our fictional insurance company.

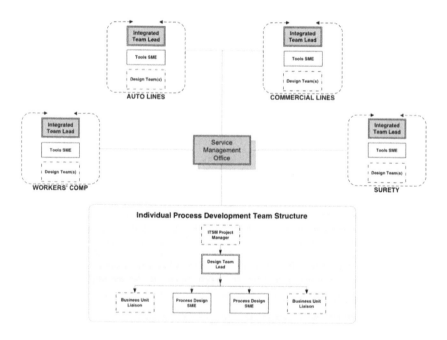

Figure 16: Integrated process development teams

Let's begin by looking at the individual team structure highlighted in the blue box (at the bottom of the diagram).

In our approach, each process that is to be developed (e.g. service catalog management, change management, incident management, etc.) is assigned to a single development team. An individual resource may be assigned to more than one team, but it is imperative that each team be accountable and responsible for one – **and only one** – process at a time. The design team is staffed with at least one process design subject matter expert (SME) and at least one representative from each of the business units that, at the time, are either significant actors in the process, or a customer of the process. Each team is headed by a Design Team Lead, who is solely accountable for process development results. The design team lead also has a dotted-line relationship to the project manager for the project under which the process development/improvement effort falls.

Moving upward in the diagram, note that each development team has a solid reporting line into the central governing authority, represented in the gray shaded box (at the center of the diagram). In this example, we assume our fictional insurance company has established a Service Management Office (SMO) that is well-suited for this role. Your organization may not elect to establish a separate Service Management Office at this time. They may wish to wait until the service management culture in the organization has matured a bit.

Of course, the ITSM Steering Committee we chartered in Step Four is also ideally constituted to fill this role, authorized by its strong executive mandate and staffed with cross-organizational representation. Whatever form it takes, this body is charged with establishing and enforcing the enterprise standards to be used by all development teams, as well as adjudicating disputes as they arise. It also serves as the governing and approval authority for all development work, wielding veto authority over any design that does not align with the best interest of the enterprise. Before moving on, we must note that some organizations attempt to use their existing Project Management Office (PMO) to fill this important role. In our opinion, this is a grave mistake, unless the PMO is chartered with similar structure and authority as the ITSM Steering Committee discussed in Step Four.

The third and final dimension of our model is an *integrated* development team that is sponsored and resides within each strategic business unit – shown by the circular dotted-line arrows. This is *not* to be confused with the dedicated development teams assigned to each process. Rather, this team provides resources to participate in process development, and advises on business unit requirements that have to be factored into the design. The integrated team lead is often the same business unit liaison that participates as a member of design teams, and is responsible for reporting back to business unit leadership with any issues that arise. A crucial role in the integrated team is that of the tools subject matter expert, who is responsible for working with all functional constituents within the business unit to ensure that functional and technical tool requirements are factored into process design. The integrated development teams are essential for ensuring that processes are designed to be interoperable across the enterprise. Ultimately, it is the business units that will suffer if there are missed interfaces or dropped hand-offs that occur between any of the critical processes, such as between Change Management and Release and Deployment Management.

Is this a perfect development model, guaranteed to win you success on the battlefield? Will multiple independent business units, each with their own profit and loss issues, always work nicely together and agree on critical design issues? Unfortunately, the answer is no – but we believe our model is better than any of the alternatives we have tried. In this respect, we are reminded of Winston Churchill's famous dictum: "Democracy is the worst form of government, except for all those other forms that have been tried from time to time."

Tools

Up to this point in our Ten-Step approach, we have deliberately avoided any detailed discussion of tools. This is not an oversight; rather, we feel it is important to be agnostic about tools while defining what the business needs, and how to structure IT to deliver those needs. We strongly believe that tooling considerations, like costs and resources, are best cast aside when discussing the "art of the possible." The business does not care what tools we use, any more than we care about the brand of carburetor under the hood in our vehicles, and neither should IT, up to this point in our ITSM transformation journey.

Are we saying that engine components, pricing and functionality do not matter? No, not at all. These become important inputs and constraints in the design, manufacture and marketing of an automobile. Indeed, IT relies heavily on automation to perform almost every activity and task that it does. The larger and more complex the organization, the more critical tool automation becomes. Customer-facing tools are especially important in creating or enhancing service value, as they act as a virtual extension of IT itself. Tool capabilities are an integral part of how we operate processes and deliver services. We simply advocate that tool capabilities be factored into *"how"* we design processes and services, and not the decision of **"what"** processes or services we deliver or prioritize for improvement.

That being said, Step Eight now requires that we consider the impact and role of tools in detailed process development (Levels III and IV). Here, we find not a sober, considered debate on the merits; on the contrary, we consistently find most practitioners aligned to one of two extreme camps. The "process purist camp" ardently believes that process design is paramount, and processes should be completely designed before considering how they will be automated. In this view, tool capabilities are treated as a constant, as in an algebraic equation. Alternatively, the "tool nirvana" camp believes that modern tool suites have advanced to such a state that processes can literally be deployed "out of the box," with perhaps only minor tweaking to accommodate special requirements. Why devote precious time and resources developing processes, when they can simply be purchased "off the shelf"?

The intensity and passion on both sides of this debate almost reminds us of a pre-Renaissance religious schism. We typically find both sides to be skillful and passionate orators, with either party more than willing to twist the laws of evidence and logic to buttress their positions. Now, we make no claims one way or the other regarding the mysteries of faith and religion. However, within the realm of practical ITSM, we believe such extreme positions present the logical error of a *false dichotomy*; neither camp is completely right or completely wrong – the truth lies somewhere in the middle.

In our collective experience working with clients for more than 30 years, we find that process and tools must go hand-in-hand. When it comes to detailed development, it makes no more sense to divorce process design from the tools that will support it, than it does to assume "out of the box" processes can meet the majority of our organization's needs. Both are false propositions, and highly dangerous. However, we are also sober enough to recognize there is truth in the claims of both camps. Process does, and always should, drive tool requirements – this is the proper order of things. However, it is also true that the capabilities of major ITSM tool offerings have progressed by leaps and bounds over the last five to ten years. It no longer makes sense to design processes and "pick a tool" at the end; it is much better to design processes with specific tool capabilities in mind, and begin functional integration testing as early as possible.

As you will see in the sections that follow, nothing replaces the hard work of defining the specific functional and technical tool requirements required to automate and support the process. Tool requirements not only feed design decisions, but become part of the formal process documentation that supports continual improvement activities. However, we do advise clients to research and evaluate tool options early in the Transformation process (e.g. Step Five: Define the Ideal Target State), and to at least know the broad tool capabilities that will be available prior to commencing detailed process design. If the organization has decided to purchase a tool suite, it makes sense to purchase licenses now, in order to conduct functional integration testing as procedures and work instructions are developed.

For the purpose of this book, we will remain agnostic with regard to tool vendors, and refrain from opining on the relative merits or demerits of any specific tool offering. We can say with confidence that most of our clients have a strong and growing preference for tools that can be provisioned via the Cloud as Software-as-a-Service (SaaS). Some tool offerings are even expanding beyond the range of traditional ITSM capabilities, to the point of resembling a Platform-as-a-Service (PaaS) offering. To site just one example, the CEO of ServiceNow described his company's offering at the recent *VMworld 2012 Conference* as follows: "Organizations deploy our service to create a single system of record for enterprise IT, lower operational costs and enhance efficiency."

Many resources are available – both public and proprietary – that can be used to research ITSM tool vendors, tool suites, and even point solutions – such as a service catalog, a stand-alone CMDB, event monitoring software, and other items of this nature. Probably the most well-known and respected independent source is the Gartner Group – specifically, the Gartner IT service support management (ITSSM) magic quadrant. The magic quadrant ranks the top ITSM tool vendors according to two key criteria: a) the **ability to execute**, and b) the **completeness of vision**.

This combined ranking results in each vendor being placed into one of four quadrants: niche players, visionaries, challengers, or leaders. In the most recent ITSSM magic quadrant, released August 2012[15], two vendors were ranked as "challengers," while the remaining nine were all ranked as "niche players." While Gartner identified unique strengths and weaknesses of each vendor, the magic quadrant indicates that, overall, there is not much differentiation between ITSM tool vendors, with the most significant differentiator being the ability to execute. With all of that being said, let's return to our standardized process development discussion.

In our Ten-Step approach, we've already addressed Levels I and II of the development pyramid. Here in Step Eight, we turn our attention to Levels III and IV, which provides guidance on the development of the detailed designs for the processes identified in your unique version of the IT Ecosystem.

Process Development Lifecycle

One of the primary reasons why the systems development lifecycle (SDLC) is so widely used throughout information technology is because it offers a structured way of creating or altering information systems, and the models that people use to develop them. The traditional waterfall approach, which was popular several years ago, has been replaced by a more proactive and nimble methodology, but the basic structure of the SDLC remains intact. This is why we have modified the SDLC framework and applied it to the application of designing structured, repeatable processes. Granted, designing processes differs from designing automated software. Yet, there are enough similarities to allow for the best aspects of the SDLC model to be customized for our use. Every step in our **Process Development Lifecycle (PDLC)** will produce a reviewable

---

15 *http://www.gartner.com/technology/reprints.do?id=1-1BS56X7&ct=120821&st=sb*.

result. This is necessary in order to substantiate completion and assure a quality product is produced.

The Systems Development Lifecycle (or, in this case, the Process Development Lifecycle) has a fair number of critics. They cite its slow development time, its increased cost, and lack of user input. We are aware, and generally supportive of, the movement to adopt "agile" practices developed by the software community, and incorporate these activities into ITSM. As practitioners, we cannot afford the luxury of being purists with regard to any particular philosophy, creed or method – we must remain agnostic. Any method that offers a better, faster and cheaper way to produce results is fine by us, provided that quality is not sacrificed. The following table, summarizing the most widely quoted strengths and weakness of SDLC comes from work published in the 2006 book, *Management information systems: solving business problems with information technology,* Post G and Anderson D L, Irwain/McGraw-Hill (2000).

Strengths	Weaknesses
Control	Increased development time
Can monitor large projects	Increased development cost
Detailed steps	Systems must be defined up front
Can evaluate costs and completion targets	Rigidity
Complete and accurate documentation	Hard to estimate cost, risk of project overruns
Well-defined user input	User input is sometimes limited
Ease of maintenance	
Development and design standards are well-defined	
Tolerates changes in MIS staffing	

Table 1: SDLC strengths and weaknesses

We would like to suggest that the PDLC has all of the SDLC's known strengths, and minimizes its most prominent weaknesses. Increased development time and cost has been brought under control through careful planning and scope management. Creation of the logical model fosters flexibility – it does not hinder it. Continual validation of assumptions and constraints has allowed us to refine our cost estimates to the point where our variances should be statistically insignificant. User input, feedback and oversight has been a constant theme through every step of the approach.

1. The step-by-step process ensures no element (essential, or otherwise) is overlooked.
2. Periodic checkpoints ensure progress is tracking toward intended goals.
3. The required validation scenarios force interdependent processes to define and agree upon required hand-offs.
4. The overarching Quality Management System (QMS) can be defined once and used multiple times.
5. Architectural standards (if and when applied) are easily integrated into the methodology's lifecycle.
6. It is easy to learn, to understand and to use.

The major benefit of this methodology is its flexibility. Should the organization wish to omit certain components of a particular phase of the lifecycle (such as defining the organization and personnel), it may do so without affecting the overall PDLC. This lifecycle gives you as much or as little detail as your organization requires. In addition, the development framework is clear, concise, simple and relevant. It was designed not as an abstract construct, but as a tool to use in the real world of process design and capability implementation.

We have created templates for each activity and deliverable in the PDLC. This makes creating and gathering documentation easier to do, and enforces established standards. Also, it acts as input to the future knowledge repository. As leadership and staff become familiar with the look and feel of the PDLC and its artifacts, communication across teams will improve because they will all speak the same language. Agreeing upon and using a standard vernacular eliminates the "Tower of Babel" syndrome so often encountered in improvement initiatives of this sort.

The ultimate goal of detailed design is to iteratively and incrementally build a *definitive library* of approved processes and service management artifacts that is unique to your organization. ITIL$^{®}$ and other resources (including this book), can help guide you through the design and development process; however, nothing can replace the hard work of actually *doing it*. Here's a helpful hint based on hard-won experience: copying process models out of a book, or replicating another organization's service catalog, simply won't work. Consider your ITSM journey a lot like having children: children are best planned in advance; they cannot be "bought" off the shelf or "borrowed;" they always involve hard work; and each one is totally unique. Despite this, in the end, the journey is worth it.

Creating standardized templates will help immensely in building your library. Note that what we are describing here is not the same thing as your organizational knowledge base (KB) or service knowledge management system (SKMS), which is much broader in scope. We are not talking about knowledge articles, incident and change records, or known errors, as important as these may be. Nor are we advocating a "physical" library of large binders stuffed with Microsoft$^{®}$ Word$^{®}$ documents and Microsoft$^{®}$ Visio$^{®}$ diagrams; this isn't the 1970s, and we don't use punch cards or card catalogs anymore. Even the most budget-constrained organization is much better served by the efficiency, search functions and information security provided by a BPM tool, or, at the very least, a content management system (CMS) or Wiki.

So, what precisely are the artifacts you should be adding to your library? As with most ITSM questions, the answer is "it depends." If you have journeyed with us this far, you should have a pretty good idea of what some of those factors are, and what the appetite of your organization – and business sponsor – is likely to be. Entire books have been written on the subject of process development, and many of the most important artifacts are explicitly mentioned (or assumed) in the chapters that follow. Nevertheless, we recommend using the following checklist to ensure your library contains all of the information your organization requires to build and manage its target state ITSM environment:

- Service artifacts:
  - Service charters (customer profiles, service demand, service financials)
  - Service design packages (service level requirements, utility, warranty)
  - Service- and operational-level agreements (SLAs/OLAs)
  - Partner and third-party supplier agreements (underpinning contracts).

- Process artifacts:
  - Process current state (maturity assessment, measurement baseline)
  - Process target state (high-level design, key goals and objectives)
  - Process model (detailed activities, tasks, inputs, outputs, data, interfaces)
  - Process policies, instructions, and guidance ("rules of the game")
  - Process governance and controls (auditing and compliance)
  - Process metrics (critical success factors and key performance indicators)

- o Process roles and responsibilities (task-level RACI including all required analyst, operator, and support roles)
- o Process standard operating procedures (SOPs) and work instructions (WIs)
- o Process tool automation requirements (functional and technical)
- o Process validation (integration exercises, use cases)
- o Process transition plan (facilities, logistics, systems, training)
- o Process performance management/quality plan (monitoring, measuring, and reporting).

Note that a key deliverable coming out of physical design is a working transition plan for moving the new capability into the production environment. This gives you time to train personnel (if required) and alert the Test, Change, Configuration and Release & Deployment teams that their assistance will be required.

All things considered, the use of a standard methodology streamlines process, service and capability development, ensures deliverable review and approval at critical junctures, enforces quality and document standards, and creates a common lexicon. If your organization doesn't already use a standard methodology, it is highly recommended that one be adopted with all deliberate speed.

We strongly advocate using project management principles and practices to oversee and manage the PDLC. Like every other undertaking where time, money and resources are being expended, it behooves one to carefully control and monitor progress. However, don't apply project management principles blindly. Never forget that project management is a philosophy of management. It is not a tool or technique. Successful project management is only possible with an effective methodology.

In summary, the actions you want to take in this phase are:

1. Decide upon and implement a standard process design framework.

2. Agree upon – and then publicize – enterprise standards.

3. Reach consensus on the broad activities each service and underlying process must execute.

4. Charter and staff integrated development teams.

5. Document tool automation requirements and procure licenses for the selected suite of tools.

6. Incorporate project management practices into your design plans.

CHAPTER 9: STRATEGY AND PLANNING

The PDLC in our Ten-Step approach has seven phases, not including continual improvement:

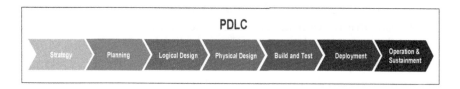

1. Strategy
2. Planning
3. Logical Design
4. Physical Design
5. Build and Test
6. Deployment
7. Operation & Sustainment.

Let's take a moment to briefly explore each phase.

Strategy

The theme of assessing and aligning strategy is carried forward in the PDLC. Although the project has already been defined, the stakeholders identified and engaged, and Process Owners assigned, there are still other aspects to consider.

At this point, the rank-ordered list of capabilities has been agreed upon by all stakeholders. While items in the list probably won't shift up or down based on criticality and importance, the project manager should analyze each capability, and assess whether two or more items can leverage the same resource, and, as a consequence, reduce the overall time to market. This may be especially true when considering two or more capabilities that may utilize the same set of tools or resources. During the testing and validation phase of the lifecycle, it makes sense to combine those common elements into the same set of testing parameters, rather than test them individually.

In addition, you and the project manager want to validate the scope of each capability. For the initial deliverable, it may be enough to deliver a basic capability, without adding expensive "nice to have" features. The old adage of "good, fast or cheap; pick two" will certainly apply at this point. Balancing what is possible versus what is affordable is a key factor in your strategic analysis.

Reviewable deliverables:
- Updated and validated strategic plan
- Updated and validated tactical plan
- Scope of each required capability
- Business sponsor approval.

Planning

The Planning phase of the PDLC takes into account the current environment, the resources allocated to the development effort, and the timeframe in which the improvement initiative is to be delivered. Your project manager will take these variables into account, and, given the constraints for each one, create a reasonable plan. This initial draft, of course, is subject to change. When reviewing with the Business Sponsor, you may be told that priorities have shifted, or that market circumstances necessitate the completion of one capability rather than another. A recent real-world example of how priorities may change can be seen in the advent of tablet computing. Seeing an opportunity to claim significant market share, your organization may decide to shift its strategic focus and make developing applications for this new platform its highest priority. The Planning phase is where you validate and "right-size" your assumptions and constraints, before moving on to the next phase of the PDLC.

Reviewable deliverables:

- Updated assumptions and constraints
- Updated estimates
- Working project plan with milestones and agreed-upon deliverables.

In summary, the actions you want to take in this phase are:

1. Assess the planned capability development and prioritization.
2. Update previous assumptions and constraints.
3. Validate the scope of each planned capability.
4. Review and validate stipulated timelines.
5. Combine development activities, where applicable.
6. Create working project plan with milestones and agreed-upon deliverables.
7. Ensure proper allocation and utilization of planned resources.
8. Build a fully loaded operational project plan.

CHAPTER 10: LOGICAL AND PHYSICAL DESIGN

Logical Design

In our considered opinion, logical design is more vital to the health and well-being of the business than is physical design. Bryce's Law [16] states, "Whereas logical information resources will remain relatively static, the physical resources will change dynamically."

If you give the matter some thought, you will see this makes sense. The logical underpinnings of your organization – its business and data components – will very rarely change. This is because those logical components are inherent in the nature of one's business. Unless the model itself changes (via a merger, acquisition, divesture, etc.) those two logical components *should* remain relatively static. Therefore, it makes sense to design information systems and processes around them.

Bear in mind that logical design is intended to support the enterprise as a whole. No matter how large or widespread (geographically-speaking) a firm may be, the design of a payroll system – to cite one common example – would account for all of the organization's divisions, regardless of location. Variations at the division level would be applied during the physical implementation of that logical design, but the design itself would not change. We have found that many otherwise intelligent and savvy analysts have difficulty with this concept. When introducing this idea, we have found that presenting the concept in terms of music helps to

---

16 Bryce's Law: *http://www.phmainstreet.com/mba/pride/laws.htm*.

make the relationship clear. Ludwig van Beethoven wrote his ninth Symphony once (the logical design). Over the years, however, countless conductors and musicians have performed and recorded various renditions of this self-same symphony. Being artistic and creative individuals themselves, they added their own interpretation through nuance and pacing, but they didn't alter the underlying structure. These musicians' individual and different orchestrations of that logical creation are analogous to the physical design.

When considering logical design criteria, it is important to keep the three types of information resources in mind: **business** (i.e. the consumers of the information), **systems** (representing the processing that must take place), and **data**. Each component has both logical and physical dimensions. When designing the processes in this phase of the PDLC, ensure that the two components – the logical and physical dimensions – are considered separately. Their differentiation is vital to successful design.

When developing the logical design, be careful to defer the addressing of how the problem will be solved technically. That is unimportant at this time. The entire purpose of the logical model is to get a feel for the structural organization, relationships, responsibilities and behavior of the various entities in the domain. Trying to drill down on things like specific data types, validation rules and storage specifics will lead you down a rat-hole, from which you may never emerge. Keep the discussion at the abstract level, and concentrate on designing a platform-neutral model that solves the *business problem* to be addressed. That is the surest road to success.

A good and sound logical model is the first step toward mobility and portability. We hear many IT professionals lament the advent of the smartphone, tablet, and Cloud Computing because their introduction into the environment creates problems for the organization. In most instances, we are willing to bet that the problem isn't the introduced device – it's the lack of a solid logical model.

Once the logical model has been created, you can then determine a suitable physical implementation of the required activities and tasks, and the required machine/human interface.

Reviewable deliverables:

- Defined enterprise information architecture model that is secure, robust, and resilient.
- Defined enterprise data dictionary and data syntax rules.
- Defined data classification scheme aligned to enterprise security policies.
- Defined policies for accessing, modifying and sharing data (within and between applications; with business partners; across all devices).
- Defined model to ensure data integrity and consistency across all devices and information stores.
- Defined quality management system policies aligned to business requirements.
- Defined project management approach that accounts for size, complexity and regulatory requirements.

Suggested checkpoint

At this juncture, we strongly encourage preparing and conducting a formal, rigorous review of the Logical Design deliverables with the ITSM Steering Committee and other relevant stakeholders, as necessary. We have dubbed this checkpoint an *Administrative Review Session*.

Through the use of structured validation scenarios, walk the participants through the model. Start from the customer's perspective, and step through the process of requesting a service – from initiation all the way to delivery. This is your audience's opportunity to "poke holes in your coat," to ask questions that have arisen in their minds, or to clarify points that may still be ambiguous. Don't fear the possibility that something in your logical design is flawed, and may have to change. Uncovering design defects early in the process is less costly than finding them in production. Engage your stakeholders, and encourage questions, comments and observations. Remember, this exercise serves to both validate the logical model, and instruct future users about the new model's functionality and versatility. Additionally, the review is yet another chance to educate your audience about the merits of the service management transformation effort.

We suggest using a structured validation exercise (either involving use-cases or user stories) to illustrate how the transformation initiative will operate – at a conceptual level – when it "goes live." Start from the viewpoint of the customer requesting or accessing a service, and follow the request through your version of the IT Ecosystem – all the way through to the final delivery. Anticipate problems that may arise (e.g. misapplied payments for services, the inability to access the website, etc.) and follow the exception process that's been designed. Make sure each participant understands his or her role, and the steps they are required to take in order to satisfy the service request or remediate the identified incident or problem.

Take as much time as is required for this exercise. Break the overall session into smaller segments, if that is called for. Avoid getting into the weeds when stepping through the process**. Do not attempt to apply technical solutions at this point.** Remember, this is a logical design validation. The physical implementation may differ. Those variances will be addressed during the physical design review that will be conducted at the conclusion of the next phase. The purpose of this exercise is to validate the logical model against the use-cases. This ensures that relevant stakeholders will have a clearer understanding of the business problem to be solved, and prevents the organization from launching potentially time-consuming and costly recoding efforts. It also provides participants with a basic understanding of the transformation effort, and makes them aware of their future roles and responsibilities.

At the conclusion of this validation exercise, all relevant stakeholders will have participated in – and validated – the overall logical design.

Physical Design

At the conclusion of the Logical Design Checkpoint, the functional requirements will be sufficiently identified such that physical implementation of the model can begin. We won't offer detailed practical advice for this phase of the PDLC because this aspect is the most organizationally-specific. The physical design will be dictated by the automated tools and relational databases that are deployed throughout the infrastructure. The data models will support and extend the organization's information Knowledge Management System (KMS).

Earlier in this chapter, we talked a little bit about tools. Now that we've arrived at the physical design phase of the PDLC, the time has come to begin developing capabilities in line with the selected tool(s) of choice. How data and information is captured, processed, parsed and distributed becomes critical at this juncture because the selected tool will have a great deal of influence on how data is structured. Another factor to consider is whether the tool will be staged and maintained in house or accessed via a secure connection to an outsourced service provider.

If, for example, the tool of choice resides in house, and is hosted on one of the organization's network servers that is attached to a Storage Area Network (SAN), the physical components (the power supply, network interface card, internal memory, etc.) must all be properly configured (and maintained) to ensure that the tool is accessible, and can support current and future capacity demands. Also, the tool itself may need configuring (with regards to access rights, the mapping of network drives and printers, performance tuning, etc.)

If your organization opts to outsource its tool selection, then the configuration may be limited to ensuring that network bandwidth and security measures are addressed.

Whatever work is required with regard to your preferred tool suite, the physical design phase of the PDLC is where these details are fleshed out.

Reviewable deliverables:

- Identified tool configuration requirements
- Tool implementation plan
- Physical database design
- Detailed data schemas (category, classification, access methodology, retention)
- User and application access methods
- Detailed man/machine interface, complete with validation and error-checking functionality
- Detailed transition readiness plan.

In summary, the actions you want to take in this step are:

1. Construct a business-specific logical design for business users, processing systems and data.

2. Define an enterprise data classification scheme and governance model aligned to security policies.

3. Create policies controlling how and under what circumstances data may be accessed (by people, systems and other data elements).

4. Convene an Administrative Review Session with stakeholders to validate the logical model.

5. Initiate physical design activities.

6. Draft initial transition readiness plan.

CHAPTER 11: BUILD AND TEST

The Build and Test phase of the PDLC is where the rubber meets the road. Developers love this phase of the PDLC because it offers them the opportunity to use new or updated tools and software widgets. It allows them to spread their creative wings while satisfying end-user requirements. Business users who've been loaned out to your improvement initiative enjoy this phase because they finally get the chance to test out the prototypes the developers design and create. In short, in the Build and Test phase of the PDLC, the time has come to actually create the capabilities for which the organization has been waiting.

There is no magic to this phase of the PDLC. To anyone who has been involved in building and testing software applications, the steps described here will sound familiar – even mundane. However, in the interest of completeness, we will touch upon a few of the more basic elements.

The first step is to prepare the facility; to establish both a development and test environment. Don't succumb to the temptation of combining the two. Developers – for the most part – are Type "A" personalities. They want to "get things done." They can't be bothered with developing something in one environment and then moving it to another for rigorous testing. They view the exercise (as well as the steps required to version the various iterations of the code) as a waste of time. Granted, there are a few developers who are exceptions to this sweeping generalization, but they are rare, and infrequently encountered.

The problem with combining development and test, of course, is the almost overwhelming temptation to "fix things on the fly." When a piece of code doesn't operate as anticipated, or when a test result displays a value outside of the acceptable range, the developer's first thought is to correct the immediate error – by whatever means necessary. The problem with that approach is that it immediately compromises the validity of the test environment. Once the test environment no longer mirrors production, then all results produced after the point when the change is made are suspect. It is the eternal chicken versus egg argument. Was the offending code corrected, or was the underlying environment changed to accommodate the code? Recall that your organization has an architectural standard that must be followed. Changing the test environment means invalidating the entire testing procedure. Keep the environments separate and distinct. In the short term, it may mean a few more steps for the development team to follow, but in the long run, the rigor will pay huge dividends down the road.

That being said, unless your organization is a multi-million dollar firm with money to spare, setting up an entire environment that supports the development effort as well as mimicking production (albeit on a reduced scale) is an arduous, expensive and time-consuming exercise. With few exceptions, most firms have neither the inclination nor spare data center space to take on such an effort. Today, most firms enter into agreements with service providers who specialize in offering development and testing environments that meets one's specifications. This option is infinitely less expensive than doing the same thing on your own, and has the added benefit of being instantly configurable (i.e. it can be scaled up or down as necessary), based on one's dynamic requirements. (A good example of this is the ability to add one or more servers to a server farm to mimic an unexpected increase in demand.)

Whether your organization maintains its own dedicated development and test environment, or leases resources from a service provider, or has adopted a hybrid approach, you'll want to ensure that the specified hardware and software adheres to the same specifications as your current production environment. Nothing is more disconcerting than migrating code from test to production, only to discover hardware or software incompatibilities.

The next step is to configure, integrate and test your suite of tools. This includes development tools as well as any automated tools used to monitor the environment, or to generate dashboards and reports. Make sure that any software used for versioning and checking code in and out of software libraries is properly maintained and administered by a trained librarian.

Once you've configured the tool suite, prepare the data that you'll use for your development and test procedures. For best results, use data that is based upon actual data in the production environment. In past years, developers and testers simply extracted a subset of the production data to use in the test environments. With the advent of privacy laws, those practices have fallen by the wayside. Nowadays, live production data is masked in several ways – either by scrambling the copied data or via a proprietary encryption algorithm. No matter which method is selected, make certain that you have the right kind of information. By this, we mean you must ensure that your development and test data contains a sampling of **all** the possible data types your improvement initiative will have to deal with.

While the above-listed activities are taking place, other tasks can occur in tandem.

If your organization is fortunate enough to have a lead developer, he or she will have the foresight to create development and integrated test plans that are designed to rigorously exercise each individual component, as well as the integration of all components across the full breadth and scope of the improvement initiative. If no lead developer role exists in your organization, assign the task to your best and most experienced business analyst. If possible, hire an outside professional skilled in creating test plans. The Service Validation and Testing (SVT) process will offer business users assurance that the new or changed service is both fit for purpose and fit for use. The SVT process is also responsible for assuring the quality of a release. Therefore, it makes sense for the lead developer and SVT Process Owner to collaborate on defining the quality acceptance criteria for the developed capabilities.

Note: While there can and should be collaboration between the SVT Process Owner and the lead developer, make sure that the lines between the two don't become blurred. Development testing is concerned with ensuring that the required capabilities operate as designed, and that they are tested rigorously enough to account for not only normal processing, but also for common exceptions that may be encountered. The lead developer is normally the person assigned the responsibility of creating component and integrated test plans. Service Validation and Testing – as previously mentioned – is responsible for ensuring that the overall *service* is fit for use and fit for purpose. We are certain that the following statement will be met with a slew of arguments, both for and against, but, in our opinion, Service Validation & Testing and development testing are collaborative, but ultimately separate, efforts.

A small number of organizations develop training plans (for both operators and users) during the physical design phase. We disagree with this approach. True, the physical design stage contains enough detail to create training plans, but, in our opinion, it is better to wait until the Build and Test phase to begin this work.

Let's briefly return to our Broadway play analogy. The Build and Test phase is analogous to the rehearsal phase of staging the play. Even though the actors have walked through the script and most of the major design decisions have been made, there are still times when the actual rehearsal uncovers something that was previously unforeseen. This discovery necessitates changing some aspect of the previously agreed-upon script or stage setting. The change is made, the actors, set designers and costumers are notified and make their individual necessary

156

notations, and the production moves on. The secret here is that all the relevant players are notified immediately. The same can't be said of your improvement initiative. By virtue of the fact that you will have disparate personnel working in separate locations, those people involved in crafting the training plans may not be notified of these "on-the-fly" changes.

Limiting creation of the training plan solely to the Physical Design phase increases the risk that key changes will be neither acknowledged nor documented. By deferring the creation of the training plans until Build and Test, you minimize that risk. Also, the major problem of creating test plans during Physical Design is the implied perception among project team members that the training plans are "complete." Once "checked off," it is difficult for people to revisit the material. It is a rare organization that has the development discipline to compare previously-created training plans with the finished end product to ensure they correspond to the end product that is ultimately developed.

Naturally, it goes without saying (although we will state it, nonetheless) that training plans for the operators who must operate, support, troubleshoot and maintain the developed capabilities must be significantly different from the training plans created to educate the end-users who will interact with those capabilities. In the former case, the training plans must approach the level of detailed work instructions. In the latter case, it may be enough to provide end-users with manuals explaining the functionality being provided. In both cases, you'll want to ensure that the plans cover the necessary components that will satisfy the needs of the audience for which they are intended.

We will address this topic in more detail during the next phase, but would like to suggest that it's appropriate, at this time, to begin thinking about (if not actually creating) the initial draft of the deployment plan. As your development effort progresses, you'll want to include the input and advice of the resources who will actually perform your Release and Deployment activities. Engaging them at this stage not only alerts them to the fact that the development phase is drawing to a close, but it will also build the necessary relationship that must exist between your project team and the individuals who will roll out the service's components. As we will shortly see, the synergy between these two teams is essential to overall success.

The last step or set of tasks in this phase is formal Acceptance Testing. This is the point in the improvement initiative where business users and other stakeholders will have the opportunity to test-drive the new capabilities. If your component and integration testing procedures have gone well, this activity should proceed fairly smoothly. However, no matter how well your development and integration testing has gone, don't assume that errors or anomalies won't be discovered during Acceptance Testing. During a client engagement that was undertaken some time ago, one of us was commissioned to develop a web-based financial application designed to examine – and highlight – transactions that could potentially violate banking laws in various host countries. Our lead developer – a young, confident hotshot – made a large wager that less than 25 errors would be discovered during Acceptance Testing. Needless to say, he found himself several hundred dollars poorer once the initial results were returned.

Many development teams view the relationship between themselves and the testers as antagonistic. This attitude is not only wrong; it is counter-productive to forging the tight relationship that must exist between the two teams. Developers have huge egos. They expect that their applications will perform perfectly – without errors. When that expectation proves false, the developers – especially the younger ones – often grow defensive, and, in some cases, combative. We have even heard developers loudly claim that the testers weren't using the end product properly!

If this happens in your organization, act immediately to rectify the situation. Before Acceptance Testing begins, prepare the developers for the very real possibility that the testing team will uncover a host of errors or problems that the development team couldn't possibly have imagined. Remind them that the testing team – largely made up of normal business people with no insight into the newly designed functionality prior to this point – is looking at the developed capabilities through an entirely different prism. Functionality or features that may seem self-evident to the developers may not even register on the end-users' radar. Use the Acceptance Testing activity as the opportunity for the developers to not only produce the best possible product for the business, but also as a learning experience for them to become more skilled developers in the future. Each team has something to offer the other. As the middleman in the equation, it is your responsibility to bring the teams together and make sure they are working toward a common goal.

In this activity, make certain that a percentage of the testing team is made up of the operators who will maintain and support the developed capabilities. While it is true they may never use the user-facing aspects of the capabilities, it is, nevertheless, important that they represent a part of the testing team. Being familiar with the ways the business units are utilizing the capabilities will enable them to better understand how to troubleshoot and support incidents and problems, when they inevitably occur.

Organizations have many different ways of conducting Acceptance Testing. Because each one of these approaches has its benefits and drawbacks, we won't advocate one method over another, but we will urge you to do one thing – log each and every bug or error that is found during Acceptance Testing, and make certain that it has been addressed prior to deployment.

This will not only act as a final checklist for the development and testing teams, but it will also be the input for the final signatory approval from the Business Sponsor prior to production deployment. It is your proof that the required capabilities requested by the business units have been incorporated into the final version of the delivered service.

Reviewable deliverables:

- Standardized development component approach
- Standardized integrated component approach
- Component and integrated test plans with clearly defined entrance and exit criteria
- Fully integrated and configured test tools
- Properly configured test environment
- Representative suite of production test data, configured to ensure privacy and confidentiality
- Coordination and collaboration with the Service Validation and Testing Process Owners
- Plans:
  o End-user training
  o System operator training
  o Acceptance Testing.
- Acceptance Testing error log
- Service and Process Assessment checklist.

In summary, the actions you want to take in this step are:

1. Prepare the test facility (development and test environments).
2. Configure, integrate and test the selected tool suite.
3. Create a representative bed of test data.
4. Build the unit and integration test plans.
5. Create an initial draft of user and operator training plans.
6. Design the deployment plan.
7. Conduct the formal Acceptance Testing criteria.

CHAPTER 12: CONDUCT SERVICE AND PROCESS HEALTH ASSESSMENT

Now that the required capabilities have been agreed upon, prioritized, developed and tested, it's time to begin the process of migrating them into the production environment. As we prepare to do so, we move out of Service Design and into Service Transition.

This phase of the Lifecycle is – in our collective opinion – the most fraught with peril, and presents the greatest overall risk to success. We have witnessed countless incidents where "there's many a slip 'twixt the cup and the lip."[17] At this key juncture in your project, you want to maximize your chances of success, while minimizing the opportunity of things going awry.

Putting capabilities into operations requires carefully orchestrating the transition of new or modified services (and supporting processes) into the live environment. This is always a dicey proposition, regardless of the conductor's experience and skill level. No matter how comprehensive and rigorous your Transition Planning and Support, and Service Validation and Testing processes, and no matter how closely your test environment mirrors production, the live environment always manages to throw a few surprises into the mix.

By this point in the Ten-Step approach, a lot of hard work has been accomplished. Milestones have been reached, deliverables have been produced, and deadlines have been met. The ITSM Steering Committee and other stakeholders have participated in the Administrative Review Sessions. Questions and concerns raised during these exercises were remediated to everyone's satisfaction. The "I's have been

---

17 *Random House Dictionary of Popular Proverbs and Sayings*, Titelman G, Random House Reference (March 5, 1996).

dotted, and the "T"s crossed. For the process designers, and other staff assigned to this project, the end of their long journey is within sight. There is finally light at the end of the tunnel.

Many project teams experience a let-down at this point. It's a common occurrence. Having worked so hard and long on the project, the team pauses to take a collective breath, before pressing on to the finish. If management – either you or someone more senior in the hierarchy – doesn't take this into account, and order a brief pause, mistakes will be made. Being this close to the finish line is going to generate both excitement and trepidation. Take advantage of this natural pause to ask yourself (and your team) some critical questions:

- "Have we planned for appropriate capacity and resources to deploy this solution?"
- "Does the deployment plan ensure the integrity of the assets being deployed?"
- "Have we accounted for every detail?"
- "Are all of our risks identified and remediated to the greatest degree possible?"
- "Did we consult absolutely everyone we needed to?"
- "Are we sure our partners (internal and external) will deliver on time?"
- "Are our communication plans sufficient to enable the end-users and business partners to align their activities with our own?"
- "Are the staff properly trained, and ready to assume their new responsibilities?"
- "Have our customers been properly notified of the upcoming service offering?"

The sample questions cited above are but a few of the thousand-and-one questions that will (or should) fly through your head at this point. You and the organization have a lot riding on this project, and it's natural for all involved to be anxious and slightly on edge at this point. It's natural for nerves to take over before launching a new initiative.

So, how does one combat this syndrome? You don't want to slow momentum, yet neither do you want the project team to commit unforced errors due to weariness, time pressure or general anxiety. How do you give the team a chance to gather itself – to buy a little breathing space – without making it appear that you're bringing the work effort to a temporary standstill?

In conjunction with the normal Service Transition Planning and Support activities, we advocate conducting a Service and Process Health Assessment at this juncture. The period between the finalization of the design efforts and the execution of the release and deployment phase is the perfect opportunity to make one final pass through your checklist.

Step Nine of our Ten-Step approach is a Service and Process Health Assessment. This simple tool provides a structured method to ensure all items have been seen to, while simultaneously giving the project team a chance to clear its collective head, in preparation for the next big push.

The Service and Process Health Assessment consist of eight major categories. Each category includes a list of pertinent questions designed to qualitatively assess relative health. The categories are logically ordered as follows:

- Process Goals and Objectives
- Process Ownership
- Process Repeatability
- Roles and Responsibilities
- Policy, Plan and Procedures

- Process Performance Improvement
- Operational Solutions Planning
- Knowledge Transfer and Documentation.

Many ITSM experts advocate assessing process maturity – either at the beginning of your improvement cycle, or immediately after implementation. This is the baseline, against which future progress will be measured. This is excellent advice and shouldn't be discounted, but, in our opinion, many of the experts have missed an important intermediate step: assessing process health. This is not the same as assessing maturity. Used in conjunction with the development lifecycle (PDLC) presented in the previous step, the health assessment is a series of questions to be asked and actions to be taken that help ensure full accountability and responsibility from inception through to continual improvement.

It may be impractical for you or your organization to do so, but we suggest having the Service and Process Health Assessment conducted by an independent, objective third party. We advocate this for the following reasons.

1. A fresh set of eyes will often catch items overlooked by persons actually involved in executing the task.
2. It gives the team a chance to work on ancillary – but equally important – duties (e.g. completing documentation).
3. It lends the assessment an aura of professional credibility (especially if evaluated by an external or internal auditing team).
4. Discovered gaps can be addressed in priority order, instead of being tackled in an ad hoc fashion.

If review and evaluation by an auditing team isn't possible (due to limitations in either timing or funding), then engage one or more members of the ITSM Steering Committee in conducting the Service and Process Health Assessment on your behalf. It bears repeating that this type of detailed engagement with the business unit leaders will build camaraderie and support for your efforts.

Let's examine each category.

Process Goals and Objectives

Processes exist to support the efficient and effective delivery of services to the business customer and end-user. They do not exist in and of themselves. Therefore, it makes sense that process goals and objectives link back to one or more of IT's strategic or tactical goals. (You will recall that, in a previous step, we linked the IT goals to one or more organizational goals.)

Questions to be asked include, but are not limited to, the following:

- Does each process have specific, measurable, attainable, realistic and timely (S.M.A.R.T. [18]) goals and objectives established?
- Are those goals directly linked to the organization's strategic or tactical goals?
- Do the established process goals fall within established risk parameters?
- Is every staff member aware of the process goals?

---

18 From Attitude Is Everything, Attitude & Motivation, 2, Meyer P J, Meyer Resource Group, Incorporated (2003).

- Are incentives and staff compensation tied to the successful execution of the articulated goals and objectives?
- Are the goals and objectives periodically reviewed and refreshed?

There are three high-level activities common to all processes. They are:

1. Define and develop the process framework.
2. Monitor, manage and report process performance.
3. Evaluate the process's efficiency and efficacy.

The first common activity – defining and developing the overall process framework – ensures that the purpose, scope, goals and capabilities for each process have been defined. Included in this activity are tasks such as defining the process's policies, its standard operating procedures, and its relationship to other processes and external entities. As noted in previous phases of the Ten-Step approach, this activity also encompasses key activities such as assigning process roles and responsibilities, defining measures and controls, and documenting data requirements (frequency, timing and format).

The second common activity – monitoring, managing and reporting – focuses on the day-to-day operational performance of the process. Its activities include generating and analyzing reports based on the metrics deemed most important to the business, and then analyzing those reports to identify problems and areas where improvements may be made.

The last common activity – process evaluation – takes a macro analytical approach. Rather than focusing on the day-to-day performance of the process, the Process Owner assesses how well the process is performing in relation to established enterprise benchmarks. Is it fit for its purpose?

Does it meet its quality and warranty standards? Is it as efficient or cost-effective as it could be? Are there any broken interfaces or dropped hand-offs with other processes? Do personnel require additional training?

As stated, all processes will have these three activities in common. Therefore, the Service and Process Health Assessment should ensure that the tasks associated with these activities have been properly executed.

Process Ownership

As highlighted in previous chapters, it is absolutely critical that each process have an owner who is ultimately accountable for the process's success or failure. Ambiguous process ownership jeopardizes the entire improvement initiative. In the absence of an owner who is accountable, process policies and standards may not be followed, performance criteria may not be met, and service delivery may be impaired.

Questions to be asked include, but are not limited to, the following:

- Has a single individual been assigned accountability for each process?
- Has this owner's role and responsibilities been clearly defined?
- Is the process owner's role and its associated responsibilities part of the owner's internal job description?
- Are the Process Owners' incentives and compensation tied to the successful execution of the process's purpose and intent?
- Has the owner been provided with sufficient authority to execute his or her duties and responsibilities?

- Has an operational budget sufficient to ensure full production support been allocated to the owner? If not, is there a mechanism by which the owner may request required or additional resources?

Process Repeatability

A successful process is one that has repeatability at its core. Every one of the process's attributes (most notably its performance metrics) relies on the process being repeatable. Without repeatability, future performance comparisons cannot be made, and, as a consequence, improvements cannot be defined or implemented. Repeatability is the Gold Standard to which every process should aspire.

Questions to be asked include, but are not limited to, the following:

- Is process repeatability a management objective? If not, there is the possibility of excessive cost due to variability within the process activities and tasks.
- Are operational, high-risk processes (e.g. Availability and Capacity Management) periodically reviewed and assessed to ensure they are fit for purpose?
- Is each process designed so that it can be scaled to accommodate future growth, and flexible enough to adjust for minor variations and unexpected circumstances?
- Are staff adhering to established procedures; or are workarounds used to circumvent the system?

Lean Six Sigma (LSS) practitioners are well-suited for assessing and making recommendations to improve process repeatability. LSS is a focused and agile method for identifying and eliminating sources of variation, as well as waste. An experienced green belt or black belt practitioner does not only help improve repeatability, but increases process efficiency as well. If you have access to skilled LSS resources in your organization, we highly recommend that you utilize them.

Roles and Responsibilities

We have already detailed the importance of assigning clear, unambiguous roles and responsibilities throughout the organization. This assignment is even more crucial when it comes to service and process ownership and responsibility. As the custodians and guardians of the services to be delivered and the processes that support them, the Service and Process Owners play a key part in the organization's ability to achieve its strategic goals. Without clearly understood and agreed-upon roles and responsibilities, the entire service implementation will fail.

Using the top-level enterprise RACI developed in Step Seven as a starting point, development teams have created a detailed task-level RACI for each process as part of the development work that has been conducted. Every RACI we have ever built has relied, at least in part, on making assumptions and negotiating areas of disagreement. Now is the time to validate the correctness of those assumptions and one's negotiating prowess.

Questions to be asked include, but are not limited to, the following:

- In addition to the Service and Process owner, have staff roles and responsibilities been clearly defined – including all analyst, operator and support roles?
- Are staff activities, tasks and deliverables clearly defined, understood and accepted?

- Have all service and process inputs and outputs been documented, along with all known dependencies, timing and frequency limitations or exceptions?
- Are supporting policies, procedures and guidance in place for swift resolution to frequently occurring situations?
- Has a clearly defined escalation process been defined?

Policy, Plans and Procedures

Policies, plans and procedures are part and parcel of the first of the three common activities. For every process, the Process Owner is responsible for defining the policies that define and control how process activities will be executed. These policies must conform to both regulatory and organizational dictates and standards. In those cases where policies are in conflict with one another, the suggested hierarchy is regulatory, then organizational, followed, lastly, by process-specific policies.

Plans are internal to the process itself. Note that this activity differs from project planning. Process plans include items such as how personnel will be trained, how the process will interact with other dependent processes, and what metrics will be captured (and how) to allow for future improvement analysis. The process plan is another way of ensuring that the process's goals and objectives will be successfully realized.

Procedures are the detailed work instructions drafted during each process to guide staff in the execution of their daily activities and tasks. Each Process Owner will define and determine the work instructions most applicable to his or her process, but, in general, the work instructions must be detailed enough for staff to follow, and to account for unexpected deviations. The ideal work instruction should contain detailed step-by-step procedures, with a graphic displaying the expected flow of information through the procedure, and an addendum containing directives on how to handle major and minor exceptions.

Work instructions come in a variety of formats. Select one best suited to your organization's culture, and aligned to the skill and experience level of the staff that will use it.

Questions to be asked include, but are not limited to, the following:

- Are process policies in compliance with existing regulatory and organizational rules?
- Are process policies known and understood by all the staff? Is adherence part of the employee's annual goals and objectives?
- Does an annual process improvement plan exist?
- If so, does it track progress toward tactical or strategic goals and initiatives?
- Are process plan milestones and deliverables clearly communicated to staff, dependent process owners and external business partners?
- Are procedures detailed enough to allow staff to execute daily responsibilities with little or no management oversight?
- Do procedures contain instructions on how and under what circumstances exceptions are to be handled and communicated?
- Are internal documentation ownership, retention and change control procedures understood and followed?
- Is there a clear understanding about how the documentation will be used for training and communication?

Process Performance Management

Later on, we will discuss the Balanced Scorecard and Continual Service Improvement in detail. However, that step takes an enterprise-wide approach. The analysis conducted here as part of this Service and Process Health Assessment will provide input into the overall service improvement plans (SIPs) described in Step Ten.

Process performance management focuses on a single process at a time, and seeks to measure whether the process is performing at the level required to support the organization's service delivery objectives. We are proactively looking for early warning signals that could indicate problems with the process, whether those problems are due to poor design, poor management or factors outside the process owner's control. In the extreme, a poorly performing process could jeopardize the chance of meeting stipulated and agreed-upon Service Level or Operating Level Agreements (SLAs/OLAs).

Questions to be asked include, but are not limited to, the following:

- Are metrics applicable to achieving business goals identified and agreed upon by the business units?
- Do management practices allow the Process Owner with high-level insight into the day-to-day operations (outcomes and performance) with limited effort?
- Have Critical Success Factors (CSFs) and Key Performance Indicators (KPIs) been established?
- If so, are they fit for purpose?
- If not, why not? Is senior leadership aware this gap exists?
- Is there an established schedule for reviewing captured metrics and taking remedial action when necessary?

Operational Solutions Planning

Operational solutions planning – as it may be surmised – revolves around the activities necessary to ensure a smooth and seamless hand-off between the development team, the release and deployment team and the operational staff responsible for the service's operation and sustainment.

Mature organizations ensure that selected members of the development team are assigned to work alongside the operations staff for a period ranging from two to four weeks after implementation. If the new service contains special processing that occurs only periodically (say, for instance, a financial services application that must reconcile transactions monthly, quarterly or semi-annually, etc.), then development staff must also be available during the first instance of the periodic processing, to help operations quickly troubleshoot unforeseen issues that may arise.

Lack of operational solutions planning is the primary reason why service improvement initiatives either run into difficulties or fail completely. When dealing with a service comprised of several dozen different components, the odds are that something will go wrong. We quoted Master Tzu at the book's beginning. This seems an appropriate time to reiterate his most famous – and for us, most appropriate – dictum: "Many calculations lead to victory; few calculations lead to defeat." (*The Art of War,* Sun-tzu). Take the time to plan for every contingency and possibility that comes to mind. It is time well spent.

Questions to be asked include, but are not limited to, the following:

- Are procedures integrated across the enterprise, where necessary?

- Is there a uniform approach to creating and distributing operational procedures?

- Has the development staff created a set of standard troubleshooting procedures for the operational staff?

- If troubleshooting procedures exist, are they housed in an easily accessible location that is known to all the operational staff?

- For services that must operate 24/7, do detailed procedures exist to ensure a smooth hand-off between shifts?

Knowledge Transfer and Documentation

Transferring knowledge – to business unit managers, to end-users, and to operations and support staff – is perhaps the most critical component of the Release and Deployment Process. Attending to this detail eases users' anxiety, ensures operations staff can support and maintain the service, and allows users to fully utilize the new or enhanced capabilities that have been introduced.

Sadly, IT professionals are notoriously negligent when it comes to training end-users how to properly utilize and maximize the advantage of their new service capabilities. Worse still, developers often spring the new capabilities on the users a day or two in advance of the service going live, leaving little time for users to become familiar with the look and feel of the new or modified service. With little advance notice, no business unit preparation, and virtually no organizational change management practices followed, what results is the birth of hostile, resistant users, who are primed to complain vociferously about every little bug or inconvenience that may arise.

As the organization's service management champion, it's your responsibility to ensure that end-users get the most value out of the capabilities you plan to deliver. It benefits the organization to make sure your end-users have the skills and knowledge that will allow them to effectively and efficiently use the implemented capabilities in support of their business processes. Doing so will reduce the number of calls to the Service Desk (especially during those critical first few weeks after the improvements goes live), and will result in happier, more motivated staff.

Questions to be asked include, but are not limited to, the following:

- Is development documentation accurate and complete?

- Has this documentation been used to prepare desktop operating guides for end-users?

- Have business unit managers been properly prepared and trained to help staff within their departments deal with the newly introduced service?

- Have Service Desk personnel been engaged to ensure they understand the timing of the implementation, and to alert them to the potential spike in service calls related to the implementation?

- Is the technical documentation used by the operations staff sufficiently detailed to allow support staff to troubleshoot and correct problems?

In summary, the actions you want to take in this step are:

1. Pause development activities to take the pulse of your ITSM Improvement Initiative.

2. Approach the Business Sponsor and request an independent Third-Party Service and Process Health Assessment.

3. Validate/refine the list of pertinent questions and oversee data collection.

4. Analyze Assessment results and remediate any identified gaps.

CHAPTER 13: ANALYSIS AND DEPLOYMENT

Analysis and next steps

Of course, after the Service and Process Health Assessment has been conducted and the results consolidated, the project team can focus its attention on remediating identified deficiencies, prior to proceeding with implementation activities.

As can be seen, the Service and Process Health Assessment is yet another tool the practitioner can employ to ensure a smooth and seamless improvement initiative.

Some of the categories covered by the Service and Process Health Assessment are addressed during the Service Strategy phase of the lifecycle (e.g. *Process Goals and Objectives*). Other categories are addressed during Service Design (e.g. *Policies, Plans, and Procedures*). *Operational Solutions Planning* and *Knowledge Transfer* are assessed as part of the Service Transition phase of the lifecycle.

Each category, properly applied and then validated, provides increasing confidence – among the project team staff, as well as with the business sponsor – that the improvement initiative, when completed, will be useful, relevant and supportive of the business's goals and objectives.

After results have been analyzed and gaps have been remediated, there is one final step we highly recommend: conducting an interactive *simulation exercise*. This step should be viewed as optional; like many of our ITSM recommendations, the value of such an undertaking depends on your organization's culture, maturity, budget, timeline, and other factors – including leadership personalities. While the shoe will not fit every organization, we are both strong proponents of using simulation as a means of validating "real world" operational readiness.

We have found simulation, gaming, role playing and similar techniques to be highly effective for a number of reasons. First, your organization has spent significant time and effort developing paper (or, better yet, electronic) artifacts – strategies and plans, service designs, process models, RACIs, etc. Some of these have been "stress tested" via administrative leadership reviews or process validation exercises. But no matter how prepared you think you are, you never know what will happen until you introduce live actors to the stage. This is often referred to as "introducing the people factor."

Secondly, in any complex system there is an element of (non-human) randomness, which cannot be eliminated – and undiscovered randomness can quickly lead to chaos. As former US Defense Secretary Donald Rumsfeld once highlighted in a press conference, we deal with both "known unknowns" and "*unknown* unknowns." Simulation exercises help uncover the latter in a safe environment without risk.

Finally, simulations provide key stakeholders the opportunity to "experience" service management in a live, interactive, real-world environment. The lead actress in a Broadway production certainly spends hours alone memorizing her lines; however, no show would come off in the absence of dress rehearsals with the full cast and orchestra.

For all the reasons above, we have found simulation to be an extremely effective and powerful method for garnering executive support, and bolstering stakeholder buy-in, at the crucial time right before capabilities go live. Simulation exercises not only uncover problems and mitigate our risks, but they vest our key stakeholders with an important stake in ITSM's success.

One commercially available example of a full-scale ITSM simulation is the "Apollo 13 – an ITSM case experience™," developed by Paul Wilkinson of GamingWorks®. We both had the opportunity to participate in an abbreviated Apollo 13 session conducted by Mr Wilkinson at the 2011 *itSMF Australia LEADit Conference* in Perth, Australia. We found this not only highly enjoyable, but very instructive and applicable to real-world IT service management situations. In today's world of mission-critical IT, loss of a crucial service can feel eerily similar to an out-of-control rocket, and, in both cases, the potential for human tragedy exists. To highlight this point, Apollo 13 was used in 2010 by the US Navy to simulate real-world ITSM and governance challenges that the Navy expected to face as the result of a large IT Transformation Program. When critical defense systems go down or become inoperable, people die.

Rather than attempt to describe the simulation experience, we will simply quote from the Apollo 13 brochure itself:

"Apollo 13 – an ITSM case experience™" is an intensive training program in which the ITIL® concepts and processes are not only explained, but also experienced by the course attendees through the use of an interactive game. In this training, real life situations taken from the Apollo 13 mission are simulated. Course attendees work in teams, playing the roles of the Mission Operations Ground Crew that aims to bring the crippled craft and its crew home safely.

We are not affiliated with GamingWorks®, and, lest we be accused of promotion, we should note that a number of ITSM simulation and gaming courses exist on the market. And the number and variety of these types of offerings seems to be increasing as awareness and demand grows. One of us participated in a Hewlett-Packard simulation, built by G2G3, titled "HP Race to Results;" this was similarly enjoyable and instructive.

Regardless of how you go about it, be sure that the simulation exercise is tailored appropriately to meet your organization's needs. Interview the facilitator/instructor in advance to make sure their method and personality is a "fit" with the intended audience. If not, insist on someone who is more compatible. As the person leading and facilitating the session, he or she will interact with all participants. If the participants feel uneasy with the leader, the simulation will flop.

Above all, be sure to get all the right people in the room – this includes not only influential leaders, but mid-level managers and key analysts, operators and support roles. Leverage your business sponsor's political capital, or, even better, convince the ITSM Steering Committee to sponsor the event. A successful simulation exercise can pave the road to sustained operational success, and build interest and enthusiasm for your final step: institutionalizing a culture of continual improvement.

Deployment

Deployment is defined as planning, scheduling and controlling the movement of releases into the test and live environments. The primary goal, of course, is to protect the operating environment, while simultaneously ensuring that the authorized components are moved into production.

Thus far, if you've followed the steps outlined in this book, you can approach the Deployment Phase of the PDLC with a fair amount of confidence. At this point, your team members – in conjunction and collaboration with the Release and Deployment personnel – will have developed a plan to identify and document all the technical, operational and usage aspects of your improvement initiative. All users who will operate, use and maintain the new service capability understand their areas of responsibility, and are ready to fully exercise their functional and operational duties.

The training plans developed in the Physical Design and Build and Test phases of the PDLC have been executed. Operational and end-user personnel have the requisite knowledge to fully utilize the features and functions of the new service. Personnel manning the Service Desk – whether in-house support, or third-party staff – are ready to respond to enquiries that may come their way.

We will not address nor delve into the various ways in which capabilities may be introduced. We assume readers of this work are familiar with the "big bang" versus phased rollout approaches. We advocate neither one. Each has its benefits and drawbacks. Every organization must assess the size and complexity of their improvement initiative, and decide for itself – based upon risk appetite and company culture – which method to adopt.

For a smaller initiative affecting only one business unit, your organization may elect to pursue the "big bang" option. For larger initiatives, a phased rollout is likely to be the best approach. The decision should be based upon a variety of factors, including, but not limited to, external market conditions, how accepting staff and customers are to new features and functionality, and the cost of one approach over another.

Take the following factors into account when deciding on which approach to use:

- How easy is it to manage the change?
- How many resources are required to build, test and implement each release?
- How complicated are the interfaces between the new capability and the existing service?
- How long will the production environment be unavailable for each release?

Whichever method is chosen, remember that installing a new set of capabilities into a production environment is always a dicey proposition. In this area, Murphy's Law invariably comes into play. There are several variations of this law, but our particular favorite is, "Whatever can go wrong, will go wrong; often at the most inopportune time."[19] This saying is more often true than not. However, this shouldn't cause panic or consternation among the team members. By following the phases of the PDLC, you've eliminated much of the uncertainty. You've done your homework; you've identified and mitigated – to the greatest degree possible – potential risks; you've checked and double-checked every item. The odds of something going wrong are infinitesimally small. Yet, you must still consider the possibility that Capt. Edward A Murphy – the Laws originator – knew what he was talking about.

We are human beings – not calculating automatons. We cannot possibly consider every contingency and outcome. This is why it is imperative that the Release and Deployment team have a well-thought-out back-out plan. Should the installation encounter trouble, or an unrecoverable error occur, the back-out procedures ensure that you can restore the system to its previous operational state. In this respect, you must think like a physician and "do no harm." If the installation does go awry, at least you'll be secure in the knowledge that business activities can continue uninterrupted, while the team puts its collective mind to work on resolving the discovered problem.

In the tumult surrounding the building, packaging and planning for the release, some project teams neglect to assign an individual responsible for ensuring that the release is appropriately reviewed and approved by the Change Management process. Nothing is more embarrassing than having all the resources lined up to execute the release activities, only to find that your team lacks an approved schedule for deploying the release.

---

19 *http://www.murphys-laws.com/murphy/murphy-laws.html* (September 23, 2012).

At this stage in the improvement initiative, it is assumed that selected members of the operations staff – those responsible for the ongoing support and maintenance of the service – will be key players in the Release and Deployment team. Remember, once the project has officially ended, these are the staff that must live with the intricacies of the system, day-in and day-out, until it is retired and removed from the portfolio. Assigning them key responsibilities during the Deployment phase is prudent and reasonable.

Lastly, make certain that your communication plan is fully operational, and that the distribution list is accurate and up-to-date. The Business Sponsor will be aware of the upcoming release, but there's no guarantee that he or she will notify other key members of the management team. This is where the ITSM Steering Committee can help. Let the Committee members know about every aspect of your release plan. Even though this information may already have been presented to them in the past, it won't hurt to reiterate it. Create a Notice of Decision, and use it to broadcast the upcoming release schedule. If possible, meet with the business unit leaders individually, or collectively, to bring them up-to-speed, and to answer any last minute questions or concerns they may have.

Reviewable deliverables:
- Verification that all key staff has been fully and properly trained
- Validated and approved release package with service assets and component relationships identified
- Validated and approved back-out plan
- Reviewed and approved Request for Change (RFC)
- Validated scheduled date for installing the release.

In summary, the actions you want to take in this step are:

1. Remediate discrepancies discovered during Service and Process health assessment.
2. Conduct simulation exercises (if feasible).
3. Execute approved training plans.
4. Prepare the environment for the upcoming change.
5. Schedule the deployment date.
6. Review and validate the back-out plan.
7. Deploy the approved Release Package.

CHAPTER 14: OPERATION AND SUSTAINMENT

Operation and Sustainment

Congratulations! The deployment has gone as planned, and your new service initiative is now in production. However, this doesn't mean that your job is finished. Even though Service Operation's function is to coordinate and carry out the activities and processes required to deliver and manage services, the staff responsible for those activities shouldn't be expected to pick them up, unassisted, on day one.

Part of the improvement initiative's responsibilities is to work alongside the operations staff to ensure that the new capabilities are performing as designed and developed. This is especially true in those first few weeks after installation. It is good practice to have a developer or two assigned to work alongside the operators to coach them through problems that may arise during the hand-off period.

You – as the ITSM improvement initiative leader – should establish that the delivered capabilities are meeting agreed-upon service level agreements. Where necessary, either you or a key member of your staff will want to manage and monitor third-party performance. This becomes critical in situations where the capabilities have been developed by in-house staff, but are now being housed or managed by an external service provider. As the person who has shepherded this initiative from its inception to this point in the lifecycle, you are uniquely qualified to pinpoint and address any service delivery issues that arise.

Also, in this transition period, you'll want to carefully monitor both the performance of the newly installed capabilities, and assess whether there is sufficient capacity to account for unexpected surges in demand.

Reviewable deliverables:

- Complete and accurate user documentation
- Complete and accurate operator documentation
- Tips, techniques, and troubleshooting guidelines for Service Desk personnel
- Performance and capacity metrics
- Compliance with service level agreements
- Third-party performance, and compliance to agreed-upon contractual standards (if applicable).

In summary, the actions you want to take in this phase are:

1. Ensure operational staff can sustain the new or modified environment.
2. Monitor activities to validate services are performing as desired.
3. Address and correct unforeseen capacity and availability issues.
4. Add or update service and operational documentation to the enterprise Knowledge Repository.

CHAPTER 15: BALANCED SCORECARD AND CONTINUAL IMPROVEMENT

Transformation[20] is defined as "change in form, appearance, nature or character."

Welcome to **Step Ten** – the final stage in your ITSM Transformation journey. If you have traveled with us through the previous Nine Steps, then your organization has indeed been *transformed* – it is not the same organization it used to be. Let's review the major changes that have taken place with our fictional insurance company:

- IT strategy aligned with Business strategy via linked goals and objectives.
- IT delivering cost-justified services the Business needs in order to scale and grow.
- Capabilities, services and processes chartered and governed by a cross-functional Steering Committee.
- Service management architecture and functional ecosystem in place.
- Roles and responsibilities defined, and aligned to enterprise governance.
- Standardized development methodology agreed and documented.
- Prioritized capabilities designed, developed, tested and deployed.
- Target operational steady state achieved.

---

20 *http://dictionary.reference.com/browse/transformation*.

Before moving on, let's spend a moment reflecting on the last bullet point. In previous chapters, we have referenced the service strategy, service design and service transition phases of the lifecycle. Design and planning for service operations was addressed in earlier chapters; nonetheless, service operations warrants a bit more of our attention here.

Just as no automobile makes it to the showroom floor without first passing through an assembly line, neither can we deliver quality services on a sustained basis without a stable operational support environment in place. Until the target operational steady state has been achieved, devote your resources to improving service operations, rather than launching new improvement projects.

Service operational excellence is absolutely critical to our long-term ITSM success. Without a high-performance service desk, our customers will not have confidence in our ability to support the services we offer. Without skilled operational, technical and applications management personnel, we cannot deliver the complex service offerings the business needs to scale and grow. Failure to manage incidents or resolve problems in a timely manner puts us at risk of breaching our service and operational-level agreements.

One of the biggest concerns for many organizations today is information security. Service operations manages access to our critical information and infrastructure; your organization's reputation and continued existence depend on the functional interoperation of skilled operators, mature processes and vital control systems (e.g. people, process and tools). Our message: neglect service operations at your peril.

But how do you know when your target state service management environment is operationally stable, and consistently producing the desired results? At what point do you stop and say, "Okay, we're 'good enough' now – let's invest in establishing a continual improvement practice?"

COBIT® provides four simple questions, which, taken together, help provide the answer. We often use these questions with clients as a starting point to jumpstart more in-depth conversation. The end goal is to help them ascertain whether or not they are where they need to be with regards to their current IT operations. The four basic questions are listed below in logical order.

1. Are we doing the right things? (Strategy question)
2. Are we doing them the right way? (Architecture question)
3. Are we getting them done well? (Delivery question)
4. Are we getting the benefits? (Value question).

As consultants and practitioners, we ask a lot of questions – and so should you. But notice these queries differ materially from both the high-level strategy questions used in earlier chapters, and from the detailed tactical questions used to perform the Service and Process Health Assessment in Step Nine. Here we are not trying to create strategy, nor do a "deep dive" into a particular process or service. We are simply trying to assess if IT is achieving balanced performance in these key areas: strategy, architecture, delivery and value. By asking these basic questions, followed by more in-depth enquiries, we are normally able to ascertain fairly quickly whether or not IT is "getting the job done." These questions are also a great way to get an otherwise reserved CIO or business executive to open up and honestly vent his or her frustrations.

With the achievement of a new operational steady state, we are now ready to dive into **Step Ten**. Revisiting our original Broadway Play analogy, we have completed the arduous work of writing the script, assembling the cast, designing the set and staging weeks of grueling rehearsals. Our hard work has paid off, and the opening night was a smash hit. The show is critically acclaimed, even garnering a begrudged complimentary review from the *NY Times*. After many months of painstaking work, including more nights and weekends than one would care to admit, you have finally arrived at your desired destination. Journey over. Mission accomplished. *Or is it?*

We hate to be the bearers of bad news, but your journey is *not* over; in fact, it is just beginning. As the ancient Greek philosopher Heraclitus observed:

> "No man steps into the same river twice, for it is not the same river and he is not the same man."

No live Broadway show will be exactly the same as the one the night before. A skilled director will continually observe the actions of his actors, stage hands and orchestra to pinpoint the smallest of improvements. Is the supporting actress slow entering the stage in Act II, requiring a special prompt? Does the paint on the background prop appear too bright under the stage lights, requiring a darker hue? Did the first chair violinist hit *two* wrong notes (aghast!) – who, may I ask, is the second chair?

In the role of ITSM Director, your environment will also constantly change. People change roles; political winds shift; strategies evolve. Companies are acquired, merged or divested. Divisions are created and shuttered. Markets shrink and new markets open up.

And, of course, technology itself is constantly changing – at an increasingly rapid pace. Ten years ago, who could have guessed Nokia would fall from grace and that your CEO would demand access to secure applications on a hand-held Apple® product? Or that your star analyst would waltz into the office one day with a funny-looking tablet device and refuse to use his company-issued laptop?

Continual improvement is the very heartbeat of service management. It acts as a critical pulse monitor on the health and well-being of your customers. It is also an essential tool to resuscitate service or process performance. Continual improvement is both a *philosophy* and a *practice* that guides us in making the iterative improvements necessary to stay aligned with the customer's changing needs.

In this chapter, we will discuss the essential role of continual improvement as our overall quality management framework for IT. We will provide practical guidance on how to plan and implement a continual improvement practice in your organization. And we will discuss how to institutionalize a culture of improvement that reinforces enterprise goals and objectives. But, before we do, let's discuss a valuable tool that works hand-in-hand with continual improvement: the IT Balanced Scorecard.

IT Balanced Scorecard

Everyone, it seems, is trying to do more with less. Noted management guru Stephen Covey once remarked, "People and their managers are working so hard to be sure things are done right, they hardly have time to decide if they are doing the right things." This is a delicate balancing act, requiring the development of good business strategies and efficient operations to deliver the products and services required to implement the strategies. Today's organizations need to be both strategically and operationally excellent to survive and meet tomorrow's challenges.

As we have highlighted in previous chapters, everything IT does must align to, enable and support the business. We do not pay lip service to "Business and IT integration" – we embrace it as a cold, hard reality. We have worked hard to reposition IT away from being a cost center, and towards a value-added business partner. To retain its partner status, IT must develop its own strategic, tactical and operational plans, including a balanced set of metrics to measure and monitor its performance. These metrics will become important inputs to guide our continual improvement efforts, ensuring we stay aligned to the enterprise strategy.

The Balanced Scorecard is an enterprise performance management system – originally developed by Kaplan and

Norton [21] as a business discipline – that has been subsequently applied to IT. It can be used in any size organization to align vision and mission with customer requirements and day-to-day work. The Balanced Scorecard helps achieve the required balance between strategy and operations, and both *financial* and *non-financial* measures of performance. It allows us to manage and evaluate business strategy, monitor operational efficiency, build organizational capacity and communicate progress. *Figure 17* shows the basic design of the Balanced Scorecard System, modified specifically for IT based on work by Van Grembergen and Van Bruggen.[22]

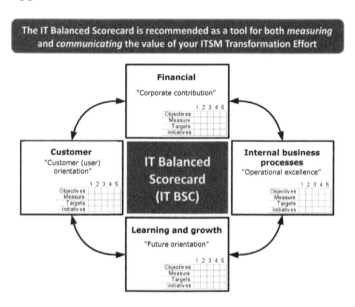

Figure 17: IT Balanced Scorecard

21   *http://www.balancedscorecard.org/BSCResources/AbouttheBalancedScorecard/tabid /55/Default.aspx.*

22   *http://www.isaca.org/Journal/Past-Issues/2000/Volume-2/Pages/The-IT-Balanced-Scorecard-A-Roadmap-to-Effective-Governance-of-a-Shared-Services-IT-Organization.aspx.*

As shown in the figure above, the IT Balanced Scorecard[23] (IT BSC) is both an internal measuring tool and an external communications vehicle. The IT BSC provides a holistic approach to measuring and reporting IT value creation to the Business. What makes the IT BSC unique is the emphasis on measuring both *tangible* and *intangible* value. Most businesses are reasonably good at recognizing the tangible value that IT provides – by measuring transaction-based services, for example. Business users intuitively understand that IT helps facilitate online banking transactions, or the processing of digital insurance claims. The same is true when a customer places a call to the service desk and a human being answers the phone.

Of course, IT does much more than facilitate transactions, reset passwords and ship PCs. To build and maintain the capability to provide these services in a high-quality and reliable manner, there is a lot IT must do "behind the scenes," which normally wouldn't be measured or valued by the business. Examples of intangible services include managing contracts and suppliers, providing skills training to staff, controlling IT's finances, fostering relationships with end-users and researching emerging technologies.

As the name implies, a well-built IT BSC is composed of a "balanced" set of metrics that address both *outcome measures*, such as service availability, and *performance drivers*, such as IT's ability to rapidly respond to new business needs. This approach recognizes the cause-and-effect relationship that exists between the investments and activities IT must undertake to "run IT like a business," and the direct performance benefits the Business receives from IT in the form of value-added services. To be effective, the number of metrics should be kept to the minimum required

---

23 Figure adopted from Kaplan R.S. and Norton D.P., ©Balanced Scorecard Institute and work by Van Grembergen and Van Bruggen, ©IT Governance Institute.

to achieve balance across the following four areas. The following table summarizes each of the four IT BSC areas, as defined by Van Grembergen and Van Bruggen.

BSC / IT BSC category	Measures and Critical Success Factors	Key viewpoints
Financial: "Corporate contribution"	This measures IT Performance in supporting and enabling execution of the organization's strategy. Factors include: strategic contribution, synergy achievement, business value of IT projects and management of IT investments.	Executive and Senior Management, Board of Directors, Shareholders
Customer: "Customer (user) orientation"	This measures IT Performance in the eyes of business customers (internal) and customers of business units (external). Factors include: IT/Business partnership, application development performance and service level performance.	Service value as perceived by Business Customers and end-users
Internal business processes: "Operational excellence"	This measures IT Performance in the eyes of IT Management and the audit and regulatory bodies. Factors include: process excellence, responsiveness, security and the cost of quality measures.	Service Owners, Process Owners, Suppliers, Partners
Learning and growth: "Future orientation"	This measures IT Performance in the eyes of the IT organization itself. Factors include: capability improvement, staff management effectiveness, enterprise architecture evolution, emerging technology research and knowledge management.	Process Owners, ITSM Practitioners, Support Personnel

Table 2: IT Balanced Scorecard metric categories

While choosing a balanced set of metrics may seem like a straightforward exercise, many organizations stumble. Why?

They try to measure too much. One major financial organization captured more than 75 metrics as part of its Balanced Scorecard effort. Guess how successful that was? In less than three months, the metrics fell by the wayside, operations shifted back into the old mode of doing business, and any progress that had been made was lost amidst the noise of the resultant finger-pointing and back-biting. Only the most relevant and impactful metrics should be selected to feed the IT BSC. Otherwise, it is nothing more than sound and fury, signifying nothing.

Once the BSC has been defined for the Enterprise, it can be successfully applied to IT in a manner that directly links IT value creation to the achievement of enterprise objectives. One of the chief challenges faced by CIOs is demonstrating how they directly create value for the Business. This is increasingly an existential question, as internal IT departments become subject to market forces including service multi-sourcing and Cloud-based services where IT may actually own and operate few, if any, *fixed assets*. In addition to SaaS and PaaS, a particularly potent driver of this trend is the falling cost of Infrastructure-as-a-Service (IaaS), due in large part to virtualization technologies.

If your organization has not adopted a Balanced Scorecard for the business (or is resistant to the notion), don't worry – the strategy work performed in previous Steps of our ITSM journey is useful in aligning your IT BSC measures with enterprise goals. In many cases, your IT BSC Key Goal Indicators (KGIs) should directly align with the IT strategic goals in your organization's version of *Figure 18* (which was first presented in Step Six of our approach). By linking IT strategic goals to business strategic goals, the Goal Linking matrix provides a direct line of sight between your IT BSC measures and top-level strategic objectives.

IT goals linked to business goals

ID	IT strategic goals
1	Establish enterprise-wide Vendor Management Process.
2	Identify all third-party suppliers and outstanding contractual obligations.
3	Account for and protect all IT assets.
4	Increase security of customer-facing web services.
5	Maintain integrity and accuracy of received client data, and PII.
6	Ensure compliance with laws, regulations, and contractual obligations.

ID	Business strategic goals	Corresponding IT goals		
1	Provide secure website services for customer order submission.	3	4	5
2	Reduce costs to outside contractors / consultants.	1	2	
3	Comply with federal and state regulations relating to personally identifiable information (PII).	3	4	5

Figure 18: Goal Linking example

To help clarify the preceding discussion, let's go ahead and take the IT BSC for a brief test drive. When we presented this topic as part of an ITSM Transformation Workshop in 2011 at the *itSMF Australia LEADit Conference*, we divided the audience into teams of four, and gave each team 20 minutes to develop a simple IT BSC for a fictional Australian mining conglomerate. We were worried this would prove a difficult task to perform on the spot with three other strangers, and so we provided attendees a sample set of BSC metrics as a reference. Truth be told, this example was sketched quickly on the back of a napkin the evening before, so don't put too much stock in it; nevertheless, it is representative of the work to be done:

BSC / IT BSC category	Type
Financial: "Corporate contribution"	**Goal (KGI):** IT budget supports the business growth strategy. **Measure (CSF):** Investment in infrastructure $+$ New development $>$ Maintenance spend **Metric (KPI):** Maintenance spend $<$ 50% of IT spend
Customer: "Customer (user) orientation"	**Goal (KGI):** maintain continuity of critical business services, regardless of location. **Measure (CSF):** all mission-critical services restored within 48 hours in the event of a major incident or natural disaster. **Metric (KPI):** defined and agreed Recovery Time Objectives (RTOs) and Recovery Point Objectives (RPOs) published for each critical service.

Internal business processes: "Operational excellence"	**Goal (KGI):** maintain an accurate and up-to-date Service Catalog. **Measure (CSF):** number of errors on the Service Catalog. **Metric (KPI):** Errors $<$ 5% of total Catalog content
Learning and growth: "Future orientation"	**Goal (KGI):** all IT employees are aware of common information security threats and countermeasures. **Measure (CSF):** IT employees provided with mandatory annual online information security training. **Metric (KPI) :** > 95% of IT employees have completed the most current version of the information security training course (including recent hires).

Table 3: Sample IT Balanced Scorecard metrics

Note that for the IT BSC, we advocate defining metrics using the COBIT® three-tiered metric hierarchy consisting of:

Key Goal Indicator (KGI) → Critical Success Factor (CSF) → Key Performance Indicator (KPI)

To our great surprise, not only did the example above spur interesting discussions, but most teams were actually able to complete a rough IT BSC in the allotted 20 minutes! Of course, in a real-world organization this exercise becomes much more complicated. Although the IT BSC is a simple tool, there is a lot at stake in the process. Organizational politics may enter the equation. In some cases, getting everyone to agree on the right set of balanced metrics may become a nearly impossible task.

Once again, we recommend turning to our old friend, the ITSM Steering Committee. This is the enterprise-level body vested with the authority and responsibility for making these decisions. As the old adage goes, "don't try to be a hero"! Your job is to provide guidance and facilitate good decision making. You are not the decision maker; the members of the Steering Committee have been vested with this responsibility by executive management, and are paid to make the tough decisions. This is also the body that must ensure the chosen IT BSC measures align to the enterprise strategy.

One final note must be made regarding the IT BSC. Once you've defined *what* to measure, you need to ensure that appropriate tools are in place to help monitor and report on performance. In a large and globally dispersed enterprise with multiple business units, sophisticated tool automation is requisite. Moreover, tech-savvy business leaders are no longer willing to accept dated paper reports and PowerPoint® slides; they demand access to near or real-time reporting via configurable digital dashboards and scorecards.

If the required capabilities are not in place at your organization, we recommend looking beyond traditional ITSM tool suites. There is growing industry recognition of the convergence taking place between traditional business systems focused on operational and financial controls, and the service management and security systems to which IT practitioners have become accustomed. Gartner [24] has dubbed this convergence Enterprise Governance Risk and Compliance (EGRC). They have defined it as the automation

---

24 *Magic Quadrant for Enterprise Governance, Risk and Compliance Platforms,* Gartner (13 July 2011).

of the management, measurement, remediation and reporting of controls and risks against enterprise objectives. According to Gartner, the EGRC platform market has expanded from a tactical focus on regulatory compliance to a strategic focus on enterprise risk management. Many vendors are busy enhancing their current offerings by adding or integrating sophisticated business performance management and score-carding capabilities. These are exactly the kinds of capabilities you will need.

To recap this section, a chief advantage of the IT BSC is that it shows not only the tangible value created by IT (for example, measured transaction-based services), but also the intangible value created by services that enhance customer satisfaction, support internal business processes, and contribute to employee learning and corporate innovation. IT BSC measures align directly to enterprise goals and are a key input into Continual Improvement.

Continual Improvement

Continual improvement is certainly one of the hottest topics in service management today, and for good reason. As the very heartbeat of service management, continual improvement should be the driving force behind everything we do.

Moreover, we must recognize that, in our enterprise approach to ITSM, continual improvement cannot be done effectively in silos. Our continual improvement approach should be designed to be cross-functional, and engage all internal and external organizations involved with provisioning and managing services, processes and capabilities.

Our recommended approach rests on two basic tenets. First, that continual improvement and quality management of IT not only fit together, but are in fact one and the same thing.

Some traditional IT practitioners who still view service management as a siloed discipline may disagree. Nevertheless, on this point we stand firm. Our second tenet is that all continual improvement efforts, regardless of frameworks or methods used, are geared towards intuiting the voice of the customer (VOC). VOC should always be the chief criteria used to analyze and prioritize improvement initiatives, and to measure their success.

One of us presented on this topic at the *2011 itSMF USA/HDI Fusion Conference* in Washington, DC and used the following example to demonstrate the important links between continual improvement, quality management and the VOC.

As the newly appointed CTO for a start-up online financial information company, the author was responsible for building and managing a global information delivery platform to securely transmit financial data and analysis to large global banking and investment houses worldwide. He set out developing targets for application performance, server availability, latency, packet loss, etc. and was thrilled to see reports showing all targets being met.

Nevertheless, angry customer calls started coming in, and, in meeting with these customers, the author soon realized that even though the applications were functional and packets were being routed correctly, from a *service perspective* customers were not getting what they needed. For example, it turned out one of the key analytical tools was essentially rendered worthless if a key data set did not get synchronized and uploaded by a certain time prior to the opening of financial markets. No one, including the CTO, understood this important link between the analytical service and the data feed.

This painful experience taught the author the importance of adopting a structured quality management approach, such as Lean Six Sigma, to rigorously analyze performance and relentlessly search out sources of variation, waste and error. Moreover, it taught him the preeminent importance of always looking at the service or process through the eyes of the customer.

What *business need* is the customer trying to meet? What are his or her stated requirements and what latent (i.e. implied) needs might exist that have gone unspoken or unrecognized? What are the minimum levels of utility and warranty that must be delivered for the service to still be *useful*? Has the service value chain been thoroughly and completely documented – are all the services, processes and suppliers the service depends on known? Is there a genuine understanding of how the service directly impacts the customer's ability to do his or her job? These are some of the questions that help us get to the VOC.

Now that we understand the importance of quality management and the VOC, we're ready to plan and implement an enterprise-level continual improvement practice that fits the culture and goals of the organization. But, before we begin, it's worth asking if establishing a continual improvement practice is really worth the investment in time, money and resources. No matter how convinced you may be, you shouldn't assume that your business sponsor or the ITSM Steering Committee will share your enthusiasm. They, like you, have traveled far on this journey and may be hoping for a respite from the turmoil. There is a real limit to the amount of change an organization can absorb, and you should be sensitive to this. And don't forget, there will *always* be vocal competitors for scarce organizational resources. Do not assume anything!

Rather than taking CSI for granted, build your case, and present a reasoned and rational argument for what you are trying to do. Let's look at some of the broad IT challenges facing organizations today, and how implementing enterprise continual improvement can help. A brief summary of these challenges includes:

- Fiscal austerity and "hard" budget constraints:

- o Your organizational mission and scope of responsibilities hasn't changed; in fact, they have likely expanded!
- o A constant pressure to do more with less, and to demonstrate measurable value.
- Compartmentalized decision making:
  - o Too many overlapping capabilities exist across business units/divisions.
  - o A powerful industry trend towards enterprise processes and shared services.
- Multi-sourcing and Cloud-based services:
  - o Solutions must address unique needs and the complexity of large global enterprises.
  - o Spurring increased focus on core competencies and incremental improvement.

In addition to addressing the broad challenges described above, be sure to include any organization-specific challenges or circumstances you feel will be helped by institutionalizing a culture of improvement. Is your organization struggling with an out-of-control virtualization project? Are your service level agreements out of date? Is the turnover of service operations staff too high? What new service or process would *delight* our customers? Here's the bottom line: your goal is to demonstrate how an enterprise approach to CSI can help you do *more with less*, by targeting resources at projects that will have the greatest impact to the customer.

No matter how strong your case, you should always anticipate being asked the "What's in it for me?" question. Based on our experience, we suggest you consider crafting a brief description of what you intend to do, followed by a statement of clearly articulated benefits similar to the following:

> We recommend establishing a *standardized*, *data-driven*, *cross-organizational approach* to the continual improvement of service and process performance across the enterprise.

Establishing this approach *now* will provide the following key benefits:

- Budgets and resources aligned to enterprise mission and priorities.
- Increased operational efficiency and effectiveness.
- Measurable, transparent results for reporting to senior executives.
- Data-driven decisions (removes the politics from decision making).

Let's briefly explore each of these benefits. Aligning budgets and resources to enterprise priorities will enable you to report the percentage of IT spend that goes directly to supporting the organization's top strategic objectives – this is very powerful! Increased efficiency and effectiveness means you can do more with less, allowing the business to seamlessly scale without a commensurate increase in IT costs. Recall this is one of our insurance company's key strategic goals. Measurable results, combined with the IT BSC developed earlier, will help us prove the tangible and intangible value IT delivers to the business. And, most importantly, data-driven decisions allow you to prioritize initiatives based on facts, not politics. The organization will never again be held hostage to a decision made over an expensive dinner with a powerful Board member who may have had one too many glasses of wine to drink!

Once you've garnered the required support for your initiative, your next step is to create an enterprise CSI strategy. Don't forget that everything you do has a price tag – there is a real opportunity cost of shifting resources and managerial attention away from what you are doing today. So, as you begin crafting your strategy, a good first step is to encapsulate some key goals and objectives. The following are three actual examples taken directly out of CSI documents from different organizations.

---

1. "Continuously improve Quality of Service (QoS) to our customers through systematic valuation and improvement of service and process performance across the enterprise."

2. "Institutionalize a culture of improvement across organizational domains and boundaries."

3. "Develop, communicate, and enforce continual improvement standards to govern how customer requirements, changing requirements, contractual obligations and evolving mission objectives will drive integrated service and process improvement projects."

Notice that the first example sets a **measurement** goal, to establish a systematic method for measuring performance in the eyes of the customers. The second example sets a **cultural** goal – it recognizes the strategic importance of institutionalizing a culture focused on customer needs. Finally, the third example addresses **agility**, strategically positioning the organization to quickly respond to changes in customer requirements. Note how all three of these examples directly relate to the VOC.

When preparing to develop the CSI strategy, we have found it extremely helpful to broker stakeholder agreement on a common definition of CSI. For instance, some organizations have adopted a continual process improvement (CPI) approach that is process-centric and excludes looking at services. Other organizations treat continual process improvement (CPI) and continual service improvement (CSI) as two separate processes. Our suggestion for continual improvement as an overarching quality management framework for IT requires an all-inclusive definition of CSI. The following is a well-written example based on the ITIL® 2007 (v3) standard:

The purpose of the Continual Service Improvement (CSI) process is to align and/or realign IT Services to the changing business needs, by improving the services offered, as well as the internal processes of the IT organization. These improvement activities support the lifecycle approach through Service Strategy, Design, Transition and Operation. Three sub-processes incorporated into CSI include:

1. The 7 Step Process
2. Service Reporting
3. Service Measurement

Our organizational ITSM Framework considers CSI as one all-encompassing process that includes the three sub-processes listed above.

Now that your organization has fully embraced an enterprise approach to CSI, and you've defined high-level goals and objectives, it's time to put pen to paper and write the strategy document. This will serve as the foundational charter for your entire effort; simply put, take your time and get it right.

The approach we normally recommend to clients is to concentrate on the "three S's":

- **S**WOT analysis
- **S**takeholders
- **S**ponsorship.

You are already familiar with performing a SWOT analysis from Step Six. In this case, you will need to consider organizational mission in light of the IT BSC, existing service management capabilities, the potential budget for improvements, access to skilled resources, and other factors. This analysis is based on the new target state service management ecosystem now in place.

Tackling the second item requires an all-encompassing analysis that includes any stakeholder organizations that may have a role to play in your improvement efforts, with particular attention paid to divisions or business units having direct contact with customers. Examples of internal stakeholders include: business units, departments and divisions, IT (of course), Operations, Finance, Contracts, and Legal. External stakeholders include customers, partners, suppliers, and, potentially, even competitors.

The last element is also the most important one. Obtaining the right level of executive sponsorship for your effort is critical to your ultimate success. The person you target for this role may or may not be the same individual as your current ITSM business sponsor. For this activity, we suggest bypassing members of the ITSM Steering Committee. Instead, we strongly recommend enlisting the support of a powerful and influential individual in your organization that has not yet been tapped for this initiative. The Board of Directors or CEO may feel that an ITSM Steering Committee member may not be detached enough to offer an objective opinion. With services already in production, they may feel as though this is a "nice to have," but not genuinely essential element. Selecting an influential member of the organization to spearhead this is a very good way to deflect those objections before they are actively vocalized.

To the greatest extent possible, try to enlist the aid of a true champion, and not just a figurehead. You are looking for an individual with a deep personal commitment to your effort – someone who is willing to take a significant career risk and invest precious political capital in your success. Take it from us, there will come a time when you need to call upon this individual to help you fight battles and remove the inevitable roadblocks that pop up along the way. Choose your candidate carefully, question him or her to assess their willingness to participate, and then make your pitch. If you have done your homework, chances are the person you target will say "Yes."

One final word of advice: once you have secured a sponsor, make sure you understand their risk appetite, and don't abuse their trust by pushing the organization too far or too fast. Communication and concentrated, coordinated effort is better than a shotgun approach.

The "three S's" is merely a suggested starting point. Part of strategic planning is anticipating sources of resistance, and developing appropriate countervailing measures. If your plan calls for the formation of a dedicated CSI team or organization – requiring budget and resources – then you may encounter one of the arguments briefly described in the following bullet points:

- Service portfolio management (SPM) makes investment decisions. *Yes, but:*
  - CSI is a key input into the prioritization of organizational capabilities.
  - Not all improvement projects result in new or changed services.
  - SPM in practice tends to focus on services and not the wide range of IT capabilities addressed by CSI.
- Service level management (SLM) determines customer priorities. *Yes, but:*

- ○ CSI is able to address the needs of diverse customers across the enterprise who may have competing or incompatible interests.
- ○ CSI, not SLM, provides a rational, transparent and fair method for formalizing, approving and funding cross-organizational projects.
- CSI is "baked in the cake" – it's already incorporated into design. *Yes, but:*
  - ○ Maximizing enterprise value requires systematic planning and a "bird's eye view" that spans the entire lifecycle of a process or service.
  - ○ This would be like Ford Motor Co. saying it plans to do away with its quality department because quality is already "built in" to its products.
  - ○ Remember that Deming said quality must be "planned and deliberate."

Every organization has its own unique culture. Take the time to consider the objections that will be raised in your organization, and tailor your responses to address the underlying cultural issues. Remember, very few men (or women) choose evil for its own sake; they merely mistake it for good. If you can demonstrate that you have the good of the organization at the heart of your argument, chances are excellent that you will carry the day.

> Congratulations! At this point, you have convinced your organization that an enterprise approach to continual improvement can help you do more with less, and better target the needs of your customers. In addition, you have developed concrete goals and objectives and created a strategy to guide your effort. Now it's time to develop a detailed plan that will serve as your roadmap as you undertake this fun-filled journey.

If you took our advice and were thorough in developing your strategy, then developing your plan will be fairly straightforward. The CSI plan is simply a more detailed and prescriptive version of the strategy. Once again, we recommend you start with addressing another set of "three S's":

- **S**cope
- **S**takeholders
- **S**tandards.

For scope, we move from strengths, weaknesses, opportunities and threats to articulating specific tactical goals and objectives. The IT BSC should provide you with a good set of KGIs, CSFs and KPIs from which to build. In this section, you also want to identify all CSI-related practices and processes that exist in your enterprise. Your plan will need to address how CSI interfaces with certain processes, and if existing practices will need to be modified to accommodate the CSI approach.

The stakeholders section of your plan requires taking the internal and external organizations identified in your strategy, and identifying specific individuals and roles within those organizations that you will be required to interface with. Specific roles might include business unit liaisons, your financial controller, vendor or supplier account managers, and, of course, process and service owners.

Finally, you need to perform a thorough analysis of all standards that influence your ability to plan, prioritize, fund and orchestrate cross-organizational improvement. Examples of standards to look for include: **organizational policy and guidance**, **regulatory and compliance mandates**, and **industry best practices**.

In our collective experience working with organizations both large and small and across industries, the most difficult aspect of any continual improvement plan is developing an integrated model. There are many industry standards and frameworks to choose from; the key is choosing the *right combination* that best fits your organization's culture and unique goals and objectives. *Figure 19* shows an example of an integrated continual improvement model developed for a large Federal government agency.

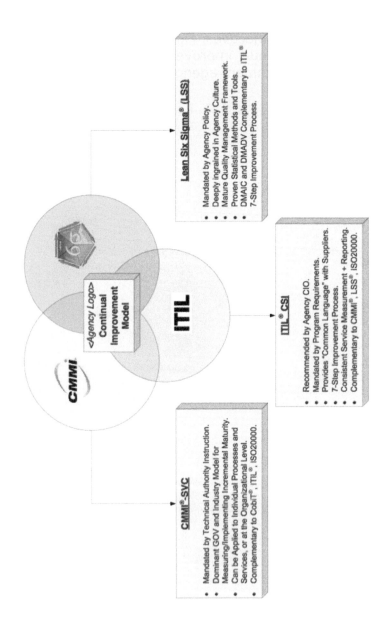

Figure 19: Integrated continual improvement model

We chose to include this particular model because it combines elements from three frameworks that we have found work extremely well together. In this model, CMMI-SVC® was mandated for use by the Agency's technical authority and was used to measure and implement incremental process and service maturity benchmarks. At the center of the model is the ITIL® framework, which was championed by the Agency CIO as a method for establishing a common language with suppliers, and to guide enterprise service measurement and reporting using ITIL®'s proven seven-step improvement methodology. Finally, Lean Six Sigma was adopted as the overall quality improvement framework, and the source of proven statistical methods and tools used to carry out the seven-step improvement cycle.

Once an integrated CSI model has been developed, you can determine the purpose and scope of your CSI effort, and define the key roles necessary for success. With regard to purpose and scope, there can be no room for mixed messages or misunderstanding. State clearly what you intend to do, your method for doing it, and the anticipated parameters of your efforts. We recommend your CSI plan contains formal, declarative statements similar to the following real-world examples:

> "This Plan is based on the leadership-approved <organization name> Continual Improvement strategy dated <dd/mm/yy>. This strategy outlines the approach to continuously improving Quality of Service (QoS) to our customers through the systematic evaluation and improvement of service and process performance across the enterprise. Service and process improvements will be achieved through a planned, iterative approach based on maturity targets aligned to organizational strategy and mission objectives."

"Continual improvement encompasses the complete set of practices, policies, processes and operational capabilities used to provision IT services to our customers. Our organization operates as a single large enterprise, and continual improvement must address each component of IT service across organizational domains and boundaries."

Before you define the specific roles needed to support your CSI effort, there is a critical governance issue that must be addressed. This is the point in the planning process where most organizations run into a major stumbling block. One of the critical success factors for your CSI initiative is designing an organizational construct that will be accountable and responsible for sponsoring and governing CSI projects across organizational boundaries and silos. *Figure 20* presents one possible solution: an Enterprise CSI Office.

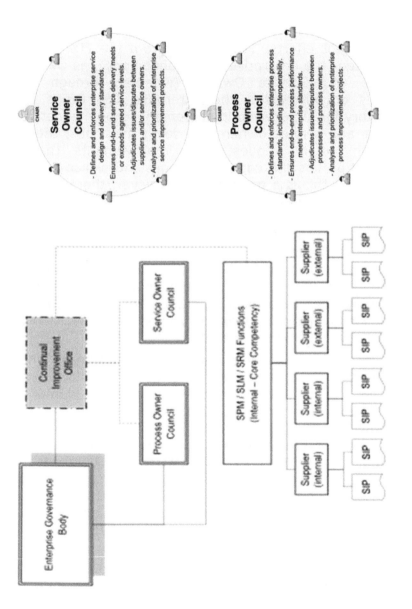

Figure 20: Enterprise CSI Office

Figure 20 depicts a semi-autonomous Continual Improvement Office, comprised of cross-organizational team members vested with both the authority and funding to *plan*, *prioritize* and *orchestrate* enterprise-wide improvement efforts. Taking input from the ITSM Steering Committee (the enterprise governance body), as well as the Process and Service Owners (whether through formal councils or otherwise), the Enterprise CSI Office is the repository for all received improvement recommendations. If process and service owners are doing their jobs, there will be many more requests for improvements than the organization has the capacity, budget and skilled resources to handle – this is a **good** thing! However, there must be a rational, transparent and fair method for formalizing, approving and funding cross-organizational improvement projects that best contribute to furthering enterprise objectives. The major benefit of having a dedicated office or team is that it will serve the needs of the many, as opposed to the needs of the few. If properly chartered and given the right scope and responsibility, the Enterprise CSI Office can be senior management's executive portal into decisions that improve services across the board.

This diagram shows only one possible construct, and, of course, the solution for your enterprise may look entirely different. Let's note some of the essential elements to consider. First, the newest version of ITIL® advocates a concept we have long recommended: the CSI Register. The CSI Register maintains an accurate and up-to-date inventory of all CSI opportunities across the enterprise, and facilitates managing these opportunities as an optimized portfolio. Secondly, note that, whatever the CSI organization is called, we recommend it be staffed with a dedicated team of skilled resources, such as CMMI®-certified practitioners, ITIL® experts, and LSS black and green belts.

At this point in our journey, you should anticipate the vital role Process and Service owners play in recommending and executing improvement initiatives. Whether via formal councils or on an ad hoc basis, these roles have the responsibility to work together to prioritize and sponsor projects with broad enterprise benefit (in the CIO's view), and not just promote their own parochial interests. The wise organization will find ways to incentivize this behavior.

Finally, we move to the large box representing the "holy triumvirate" of critical ITSM processes and functions responsible for identifying and coordinating improvement opportunities in concert with both internal and external suppliers. Note that for service portfolio management (SPM), service level management (SLM), and supplier relationship management (SRM) to be effective, it is essential that detailed service improvement plans (SIPs) be maintained for every live service on the service catalog.

Once the Enterprise CSI Office (or equivalent organization or team) has been designed, it is finally time to define and staff the roles required to execute our CSI Plan. At this point in your journey, some of these roles should already exist. Process and service owners are two prime illustrations. It goes without saying that the following roles and descriptions are provided as examples only; as the ITSM General, it is your responsibility to see that the right roles are defined and staffed with skilled personnel to successfully execute your battle plan.

As part of the CSI Plan, we recommend including explicit language to help put roles in strategic context, such as the example provided below:

> "A number of key roles are required to institutionalize a culture of improvement and enforce common "rules of the game" across enterprise domains and organizational boundaries. The implementation of CSI practices and the execution of CSI projects is a joint responsibility of all Business Unit leaders, and success will greatly depend on strong executive sponsorship at the top. *Table 4* describes the key roles and responsibilities for <organization name> CSI.

The CSI Office will work to fill key roles in concert with human resources and in accordance with the organization's enterprise Governance Model. New positions, if required, will be added in accordance with published policy:"

Role	Description/responsibilities
Continual Service Improvement Owner	The named individual accountable for Continual Improvement results across the enterprise. • Responsible for prioritizing and recommending service improvements based upon enterprise goals and objectives. • Liaison to Process Owner and Service Owner Council(s). • Final arbiter of cross-domain disputes, conflicts and issues. There should be only one CSI Owner for the enterprise.
Continual Service Improvement Manager	Named individual responsible for planning, orchestrating and supervising an integrated program of continual improvement to ensure efficiency and effectiveness of enterprise IT services and underpinning processes. The CSI Manager works in collaboration with, and in support of, Process Owners, Process Managers, Service Owners and Service Managers, as each has accountability and responsibility for continual improvement of their process or service. • The CSI Manager is responsible for ensuring service measurement and reporting across the enterprise.
Continual Service Improvement Analyst	The individual(s) responsible for gathering service and process performance data across multiple organizations. • The CSI Analyst is responsible for consolidated data analysis and reporting, including identifying trends and assessing impact.

	• The CSI Analyst makes recommendations to the CSI Manager regarding the design and prioritization of CSI projects.
Service Owner	The named individual accountable for the proper design, execution and improvement of one or more services within the enterprise service portfolio.
	• The Service Owner is vested with accountability for all aspects of the end-to-end strategic management of the service through its entire lifecycle.
	• The Service Owner is the single point of contact for service performance, regardless of the underpinning technology components or processes supporting that service.
	• The Service Owner is the primary point of contact for all organizations utilizing the service and has the responsibility for ensuring the service is continually improved.
	There should be only one Service Owner for each IT service.
Service Manager	The individual responsible for managing the development, implementation, evaluation and on-going management of new and existing services in the enterprise service portfolio.
	• The Service Manager is the focal point for driving all service decision-making processes, managing service objectives in alignment with the Service Owner's strategic goals, and managing the performance of internal and external service providers.
	• The Service Manager leads cross-organizational planning and communication to capitalize on financial improvement opportunities, while ensuring the service meets customer needs.
	• A Service Manager may manage one or more services.

Table 4: Recommended CSI roles

A well-crafted plan requires numerous elements, and careful deliberation over what must be included for completeness, and what may be excluded for brevity. At a minimum, we recommend your CSI Plan addresses the following six additional elements. Rather than discussing these in detail, we have briefly summarized them:

1. **Maturity Model:** This section describes how iterative process and service maturity targets will be developed based on organizational maturity targets and IT Capability "triggering events," using a methodology such as CMMI-SVC®.

2. **Process Model:** This section describes the enterprise process to define and govern CSI across the enterprise. This may be an adaptation of the ITIL® 7-Step improvement model, an adoption of Lean Six Sigma DMAIC and DMADV, some combination of these two models, or an altogether proprietary model.

3. **Project Selection:** This section describes how continual improvement projects will be defined, prioritized, approved, funded and implemented. Clear evaluation and decision criteria should be defined and used in conjunction with standardized tools, such as a project prioritization matrix, project analysis tool, etc.

4. **Metrics:** This section describes how enterprise standard process, service and technology metrics will be developed to enable the achievement of enterprise CSI objectives. Although our customers are primarily concerned with service metrics, a comprehensive quality management approach to CSI requires monitoring, measuring and reporting on process and technology metrics as well.

5. **Auditing:** This section describes the creation of an auditing plan to conduct periodic and ad hoc audits of

process and service performance as an input into enterprise CSI planning and remediation activities.

6. **Tools:** This section describes the approach to establishing the tool capabilities required to sufficiently automate service measurement and reporting activities across the enterprise. CSI-related tool capabilities include, but are not limited to, distributed databases and data mining software, monitoring and statistical analysis tools, auditing tools, and reporting dashboards and scorecards.

During the course of our client work, we have developed a number of templates that directly support the goals of implementing an enterprise continual improvement practice and institutionalizing a culture of improvement. Plans are currently in the works for making these commercially available (as well as the other templates mentioned throughout the course of this book). These templates include:

- *CSI Strategy template*, including instructions and sample boilerplate text
- *CSI Plan template*, including instructions and sample boilerplate text
- *CSI Project evaluation template*, including goals, metrics and the Business Case
- *CSI Project prioritization matrix*, including customizable evaluation criteria
- *CSI Project analysis tool*, including customizable weighting criteria and financials.

In summary, the actions you want to take in this step are:

1. Verify the target operational steady state has been achieved.
2. Develop and implement an IT Balanced Scorecard (IT BSC):
   - Create measures that show that IT's tangible and intangible to the business.
   - Define a balanced set of metrics across the four key areas.
3. Position Continual Improvement as an overall Quality Management approach focused on the voice of the customer (VOC).
4. Create an enterprise Continual Improvement (CSI) Strategy:
   - Define a standardized, data-driven, cross-organizational approach to continual improvement across the enterprise.
   - Define key goals and objectives in alignment with enterprise strategy.
   - Establish strong executive sponsorship and stakeholder buy-in.
   - Anticipate argument against the CSI effort and develop countermeasures.
5. Create an enterprise Continual Improvement (CSI) Plan:
   - Define the detailed Scope, Stakeholders, and Standards (three S's).
   - Develop an integrated CSI model combining "best of breed" frameworks.
   - Design an organizational construct for a dedicated CSI Office/Team.
   - Define and staff key CSI roles to execute the Plan.
   - Define the Maturity Model, Process Model, Project Selection, Metrics, Auditing and Tools.
6. Use standardized templates to document, analyze, prioritize and manage enterprise improvement opportunities.

CHAPTER 16: PUTTING IT ALL TOGETHER

As we stated at the book's outset, our Ten-Step approach is not intended to be the prescriptive end-all and be-all of IT Service Management Improvement Initiatives. Rather, it is a series of simple, yet focused, steps that we have found useful to follow over the course of our respective careers.

In our collective opinion, this is a fascinating time to be an ITSM Practitioner or Decision Maker. After a period of stagnation, we believe industry – across the board – is poised to begin a new phase of innovation and creativity. In order to do so, they will – out of necessity – turn to their IT departments. Information Technology is the engine driving most – if not all – of the initiatives businesses wish to pursue. And whether those IT departments are part of the organization they are trying to help, or are valued business partners that have been brought in for a specific purpose, matters very little. **Every** business depends upon its Information Technology assets. The differentiation between successful and unsuccessful organizations is in how effectively each one leverages those assets.

We started formulating and using this approach because we discovered that no single framework was adequately sufficient to meet the needs of today's complex, and highly diversified, transnational organizations. Why, we asked ourselves, should our attention be confined to the strictures of one framework, when there were a multitude from which to choose? As practitioners, we naturally gravitated toward ITIL®, but quickly recognized that COBIT®, Lean Six Sigma and other frameworks enhanced the offerings in our consultant toolbox. So we decided to cobble together our own unique approach. Our first attempts, however, were – frankly – scatter-shot. There were many reasons for our initial failures, but we soon discovered that the primary culprit was the absence of a comprehensive, coherent strategy, supported by nimble tactical plans. We found that many organizations – driven largely by external factors –

focus on very short-term goals. In their quest to meet "expectations," executive leaders rarely look beyond the upcoming quarterly numbers. This "attention deficiency syndrome" is responsible for many of the problems bedeviling organizations today.

The astute reader will have noticed that we spend a lot of time talking about strategy and preparation. We have said it before, and will say it again: tactics without strategy is nothing more than sound and fury – signifying nothing. You must know your destination before you embark upon your journey. Convincing your CEO to establish a three to five-year strategy may be difficult, but it will pay tremendous dividends in the long term.

The Ten-Step approach is presented as a logical progression, with one step building upon the successes of the ones that have gone before. However, it isn't strictly necessary to follow the Ten-Step approach in lock-step order. In fact, one of the most appealing aspects of the method is its flexibility. Your organization may be more mature in certain aspects of service management than in others. For example, your firm may already have clearly defined roles and responsibilities in place, which are known and accepted by everyone throughout the enterprise, but may have a crying need to establish a cross-representational body to render decisions. In that case, you would apply the principles outlined in Step Four before doing anything else.

Every organization is different, and, therefore, each one must focus first on its pain points and take care of the particular problems bedeviling it. Only after this initial triage has been conducted and corrective action taken, can the organization turn its attention to fixing the underlying organic problem that caused the initial headache in the first place. If Step Four (or Six, or Eight) of our approach is where you feel it necessary to begin, then, by all means, do so. No one will fault you for it.

We – to the greatest degree possible – aligned our steps to the various phases of the ITSM Lifecycle. Developing the initial Business Case, conducting the service inventory, carrying out a current state analysis, and then crafting and recommending a prescriptive course of action all fall within the Service Strategy phase of the Lifecycle.

In the Service Design phase, we addressed assembling and establishing the ITSM Steering Committee, defining the target state (via the IT Ecosystem), and engaged in some hard-nosed negotiations regarding what could and could not be accomplished, given the constraints of time, resources and money. In this phase, we also decided upon tools, defined a standard process development methodology, and gained approval on a Logical and Physical Design.

In addition to the standard Service Level and Operating Level Agreements, Service Design Package and Deployment Plan – that one would typically find included under the umbrella of Service Transition – we have also included the Service and Process Health Assessment checklist.

Because this book focuses on designing and introducing a service management culture into an organization, Service Operation falls outside the purview of our Ten-Step approach. That being said, the departments and individuals responsible for ongoing support and maintenance may find artifacts such as the Notice of Decision, Process Standard Operating Procedures and Work Instructions useful. Encourage adoption and use. Doing so will ease communication.

Even though Operation and Sustainment has its own set of issues and concerns, never forget that the data collected during the delivery of the services will be used to advance the improvement of existing services, and be the seeds for the genesis of new services. The ITSM Lifecycle – like life itself – is an unbroken circle, with each phase interacting with and influencing one another. As the ITSM General, instill in the organizational mindset the importance of collecting and analyzing operational data to ensure that the business is getting the value it expected for the cost it expended.

Once that data has been gathered and analyzed, use the tips and techniques contained in the chapter dedicated to Continual Service Improvement to further refine your service offerings.

The fundamental theme of this work has been the necessity of partnering with executive leadership and the departmental unit heads in order to help them solve the *business* problems facing them.

Ask the right questions. COBIT® suggests there are four critical ones:

- Are we doing the right things?
- Are we doing them the right way?
- Are we getting them done well?
- Are we getting the benefits?

The first question is strategic. Are the organization's investments in line with its vision and business principles? If not, these funds aren't contributing to achieving the organization's stated goals and objectives. Realigning the investment mix or restating the goals (whichever makes the most *business* sense) is in order. Do those same investments enable genuine value at an affordable cost, and with an acceptable level of risk? If not, then the investment should be discontinued, or the risk modified, to bring it in line with established parameters. Does the organization know and understand its total investment in its Information Technology department? Is that investment paying expected dividends? If not, why not?

The second query can be thought of as the architecture question. Are the investments in line with the enterprise's architecture, and are they consistent with the architectural principles and standards? In other words, are dollars being spent on new technology that benefits only a small percentage of enterprise users? If so, does the return on investment meet or exceed expected standards? If not, then analysis is required to understand why the gap exists, and whether adjustments need to be made.

The third enquiry is the delivery question. How well are the services being delivered to the customers? Is it disciplined and effective? Are the services delivered reliably and securely? Do proper channels exist to account for required changes to the services? When issues or problems arise, are they quickly and efficiently resolved? Does the organization have the right number of *competent*, trained staff to meet current and future demand?

The last question is – of course – the value question. Does everyone in the organization have a shared understanding of what constitutes value? Without this baseline, the organization runs the very real risk of different business units chasing the wrong types of opportunities. Is there a clear understanding of the expected benefits from new or ongoing investments?

These are questions every CIO or IT Service Manager should be able to answer. When closeted with the business unit heads, or the CEO/CFO, the conversations will always be business-based, and will be focused on achieving one or more of the organization's goals. When you can show how each process or function under your administration adds value to the business, you will have achieved true rapport with executive leadership. No feeling is more satisfying.

Once you begin to think like one of your business colleagues, you'll be able to objectively assess which aspects of the IT department are providing genuine value, which ones are "delighters" (i.e. nice to have, but not essential), and which ones have little or no value at all. With that mindset, you won't need the business to tell you what to retain and what to retire. You'll already know, and, through this knowledge, you'll be able to drive costs down because your department won't be spending money on unwanted and unnecessary baggage. You'll be proactively developing a list of rank-ordered IT capabilities that will be satisfying to the business.

Of course, every cost made in one area means foregoing an opportunity in another. As much as one would like, we cannot have it all. There will always be trade-offs – they are part and parcel of the business world, and an integral component of any negotiation. When developing the enterprise heat map and deciding upon the investment portfolio, make sure your leadership is considering all three prongs of the business: that which is required to *operate* the business on an on-going basis; that which is required to **grow** the business; and that which is required to *transform* the business. The budget must be balanced across all three categories. IT must assess the impact on its internal bottom line, and then ensure they are positioned well – now, **and** in future.

When designing the enterprise architecture model, keep these four service design criteria in mind:
1. Availability
2. Capacity
3. Security
4. Resiliency.

The first two criteria should be self-evident. In today's day and age, customers not only expect the service to be available 24/7 – they also expect they won't be turned away because demand has exceeded capacity. Customers may forgive one or two missteps in these areas, but continued problems will cause them to seek out other service providers.

Security is a hot topic today, and will continue to be so in the foreseeable future. Customers want assurance that the information they provide is secure from unauthorized access – especially from those external to the organization to which they have entrusted their confidential information. Failure to adequately address this criterion will not only cause you to lose current and potential customers, but may also brand you unfavorably in the court of public opinion, in addition to running the danger of monetary fines or other forms of punitive action.

Resiliency, of course, speaks of the ability of your architectural design to evolve as necessary to meet changing market conditions and technological advances. An enterprise architectural model that is robust and resilient is preferable to one that is static. A system is complicated when it has many components, each one of which is intricate, convoluted, difficult to understand, and requires specialized skill and knowledge. A model is said to be complex when it has many components, each one of which is simple, straightforward and easy to understand. Your enterprise architectural model can be either complex or complicated. *Complex is better.*

Lastly, develop your architectural principles, policies and guidelines first. Then – and only then – develop target state architectures for each business unit or geographical subsidiary. This information, coupled with the analysis of the capabilities, systems and services required to achieve the organization's aims, is used to decide **what** to build. *How* one goes about building it is a separate decision.

Similarly, your service management architecture – the "stuff" that sits atop the enterprise architectural model – must meet the same four criteria. It's every bit as important for internal staff to consider the service management aspects of delivering services as it is for an external service provider. The service management architecture is required to develop standard, repeatable processes. Properly crafted, it defines the key relationships and interfaces between the component pieces. Effective "seam management" ensures there are no dropped or missed hand-offs, and contributes to good organizational oversight and administration. You may have the best enterprise architectural model on the face of the planet, but if the process it supports isn't as well-planned and designed, you risk the failure of the entire improvement initiative. Keep in mind that organizational change management is the unmentioned elephant in the room. Keep the size and scope of the effort in mind, and continually re-examine your assumptions.

A valuable exercise when educating staff on the various roles and responsibilities inherent in a service management culture is to engage in a role-playing simulation. The discussion in Step Nine about **Apollo 13 – an ITSM case experience**™ is a good example of an activity that can be conducted to familiarize users with the implications of the impending service enhancement. Like other games of its ilk, this role-playing scenario underscores the importance of each person's role, and how it relates to others within the organization. It helps participants understand segregation of duties, and bolsters executive and staff buy-in. As you and your organization work through the enterprise RACI exercise, you may wish to consider using a tool such as this to foster discussion.

This role-playing or gaming supports the entire organizational change management (OCM) process, which is the thread running through your entire service management improvement initiative. At the risk of being repetitive to the point of boredom, OCM can't be given short shrift. It is as vital a component as your business plan. Human beings dislike change. They are most comfortable with the familiar – with the tried and true. Any type of change introduced into the environment must be carefully managed and coordinated. Constant communication is the key to success here. Whenever possible, form coalitions in the business units that will support and champion your efforts, and make them a virtual part of your team. Include them on all internal team communications, and check in with them periodically. They will be your staunchest allies, and will help to socialize the upcoming changes within their respective areas.

Ideal service management requires a *balanced* approach to people, processes and technology. Too many organizations tip the scales toward one leg of the stool (i.e. technology) to the detriment of the other two. Doing so is self-defeating.

The people dimension concerns itself with organizational change management and the cultural initiatives inherent to it. Among other activities, it includes strategic and tactical communication plans, skills development and role-based training.

The process dimension encompasses the governance framework, the management controls that must be established and enforced, and the assessment – now and over time – of the maturity of the organization.

The technology dimension concerns itself with customizing and integrating the licensed tool suite, and applying best-of-breed practices to the industry of IT to satisfy the organization's needs, wants and desires.

What now?

Service management is equal parts art and science. It is the art of sensing what needs to be accomplished, and then applying the science to respond appropriately. How each organization does this is unique to their culture and climate. We cannot prescribe how you, the reader, should sense and respond. The Four Keys listed below were some of the very first things we stressed. We repeat them here.

Avoid the "big bang" approach: ITIL® is specifically designed as a framework for achieving incremental and continuous improvement – not overnight results. It is better to have many small wins than one massive failure.

Establish strong Executive support: In order to succeed, you must have strong and consistent executive support. Having it gives you the authority and budget to proceed. Without it, you are simply another voice, crying in the wilderness. Find a business sponsor who shares your passion and insight and use him or her effectively.

Invest in required resources: IT service management is a long-term investment in the transformation of the management of IT. Many organizations fail to make the necessary investment in infrastructure, automated tools, and in training and educating staff. This is short-sighted, and self-defeating. Staff resources are an organization's most precious asset. It is responsible for operating and sustaining the environment. Without trained, motivated staff, the transformation will either fail to deliver expected results, or will collapse under its own weight. Neither scenario is attractive.

Manage organizational change: Position the ITSM improvement initiative as a strategic goal that is every bit as important as expanding market share. Paint a picture of what the new model will look like, and then chart a path to move from where you are to where you want to be. Nurture the fearful, and empower the trailblazers.

Monday morning, 9:00 a.m

You've reached the end of this book. You're fired-up and enthusiastic. When you go into your office on Monday, what's the first thing to do after your morning coffee? We suggest the following:

- Sit down at your desk and think about a *business problem* that needs to be solved.
- Undertake a realistic assessment of the situation and the environment.
- Do a preliminary SWOT analysis.
- Prepare a preliminary estimate of costs versus benefits.
- Assess the risks and opportunities inherent in your approach.
- Seek out and obtain executive sponsorship and support.

Assuming you've successfully found an executive willing to sponsor your efforts, over the following 90 to 100 days conduct an in-depth current state inventory of your services and resources. Engage your business partners, explain what you're trying to do, and cultivate their support and buy-in. Present the findings to your sponsor, and then to the organization's senior or executive leadership. Present it as a potential investment opportunity that will pay dividends in the short, medium and long-term.

> **Note:** Don't take longer than 90 to 100 days to conduct your inventory and engage business partners. During this initial stage, you want to move swiftly, so that you can establish an IT service management "beachhead." Nothing kills a promising concept more quickly than dragging the process out interminably. What you come up with doesn't have to be perfect; it has to pass the twin tests of reasonableness and attractiveness. If you can prove that, you will gain the approval and support you require.

Lastly, keep these five edicts in mind:

- Hire *smart* people – if you're the smartest person in the room, then it's time to find a different room.
- Keep the momentum going – slowing down is okay, stopping is not.
- Many **small wins** are preferable to one major victory – small wins build credibility and encourage people to jump on the bandwagon. Everyone wants to associate with a winner.
- Plan for, communicate and embrace change – it's life's only constant.
- Never forget that your initiative is a journey – **not** a destination.

Good luck!

Angelo Esposito
Timothy Rogers

APPENDIX A: BUSINESS PLAN TEMPLATE

Proposal Name

Business Sponsor:

Program Manager:

Prepared: {Date}
Revision: {Revision Number}

	Name	Signature	Date
Approved By	\<Name Title, Department>	Signature of approving Director or Assoc. Director	
Approved By	\<Name Title, Department>	If required, additional signature from the Steering Committee Chair or Director of impacted or shared function	
Approved By	\<Name, Title, Department>	Business Sponsor Signature	

Appendix A: Business Plan Template

[Organizational Logo or Header Inserted Here]   [Document Identifier Inserted Here]

Table of Contents

Appendix A: Business Plan Template

Appendix A: Business Plan Template

Executive Summary

Proposal Context

This is a brief statement specifying the business problem to be solved, or the business opportunity to be exploited.

Business Case Synopsis

This is a statement briefly outlining the:

- Value the proposal will deliver
- Estimated duration for delivery
- Risk, financial return and strategic alignment scores
- Dependencies
- Key risks.

Appendix A: Business Plan Template

Cost/Benefit Information

Financial Benefits

This section contains detailed benefit information.
- Financial benefits (full economic life cycle, best case, worst case, most likely)
- Description quantifying the benefits, including cash flow (cash in and cash out)
- Description of measurement techniques that will be used (i.e. revenue generation, cost avoidance, increased efficiency)
- Assumptions
- Constraints
- Market and/or timing sensitivity
- Accountability.

Financial Costs

This section contains detailed cost information.
- Financial costs (full economic life cycle, best case, worst case, most likely)
- Total commitment costs (i.e. how much to fund this proposal)
- Assumptions
- Constraints
- Accountability.

Non-Financial Benefits

This section is optional. If it is included, the following items should be addressed:
- Description quantifying the benefits
- Description of measurement techniques that will be used
- Assumptions
- Constraints
- Accountability.

Non-Financial Costs

This section is optional. If it is included, the following items should be addressed:
- Description quantifying the benefits
- Description of measurement techniques that will be used
- Assumptions
- Constraints
- Accountability.

Appendix A: Business Plan Template

Risk Analysis

This section should include all identified risks to the proposed initiative, including mitigation strategies for those risks.

Organizational / Department Impacts

This section details any projected business/operational changes that must take place if the proposal is approved and launched. Identify:

- Affected stakeholders
- How change will be communicated & implemented
- Detail underlying costs that will be incurred (this should be included in the financial cost section)
- Impact of not undertaking the proposal (i.e. what is the opportunity cost).

Proposal Approach and Milestones

Possible Approaches
This section lists the analyzed courses of action (COA) for the proposed initiative.

Selected Approach
This selection recommends one of the analyzed COAs described above.

Projected Milestones
This section lists project milestones, and associated deliverables. To the greatest extent possible, milestones should be linked to specific deliverables.

Critical Success Factors
This section lists those factors that are critical to the success of the proposed initiative.

Identified Dependencies
This section lists all known dependencies.

Enterprise Architecture Compliance
This section addresses (where applicable) compliance with enterprise architectural standards, or requests exception to those standards.

Security Policy Compliance
This section lists adherence to established security policies.

Key risks
This section lists the key (not all) risks that may impact or impede the proposed initiative.

Appendix A: Business Plan Template

Proposal Execution Plan

Proposed Execution Plan

Description of project

Planning assumptions

Technology impact (if any)

Staffing requirements (current and future state)

Estimated schedule and costs

High-level Benefits

Risk Management Plan

Change Management

Change Management, as defined here, relates to underlying changes that must be made to business requirements, processes or procedures that will be necessary to support the proposed initiative. This section of the Business Plan is **not** intended to address how changes to the overall project are introduced, analyzed, and either accepted or rejected.

Governance Structure (i.e. required controls)

Key risks

Realizing Benefits

Benefits Description (projected life, full economic life cycle, best case, worst case, most likely)

High-level Financial Benefits

Key Risks

Appendix A: Business Plan Template

Appendices

Detailed cost/benefit model

Detailed project plan

Detailed risk management plan

Detailed benefits realization plan

Full Return on Investment calculation

REFERENCES

SWOT Analysis

(*SWOT Analysis for Management Consulting*, Humphrey A, SRI Alumni Newsletter (2005)

(*SWOT Analysis: It's Time for a Product Recall – Long Range Planning*, Westbrook T and Hill R, Long Range Planning (1987)

Management Processes and Functions, Armstrong M, London CIPD (1996)

Project Management

Practice Standard for Work Breakdown Structures, Second Edition, Project Management Inst. (2006)

(*Effective Work Breakdown Structures*, Haugan G T, Management Concepts, Vienna (2002)

Business Process Modeling

Business Process Management's Success Hinges on Business-Led Initiatives, Gartner (2005)

Organizational Change Management

(*Leading Change*, Kotter J, Harvard Business Press (1996))

ITG RESOURCES

IT Governance Ltd. sources, creates and delivers products and services to meet the real-world, evolving IT governance needs of today's organisations, directors, managers and practitioners.

The ITG website (*www.itgovernance.co.uk*) is the international one-stop-shop for corporate and IT governance information, advice, guidance, books, tools, training and consultancy.

www.itgovernance.co.uk/itsm.aspx is the information page on our website for ITSM resources.

Other Websites

Books and tools published by IT Governance Publishing (ITGP) are available from all business booksellers and are also immediately available from the following websites:

www.itgovernance.eu is our euro-denominated website which ships from Benelux and has a growing range of books in European languages other than English.

www.itgovernanceusa.com is a US$-based website that delivers the full range of IT Governance products to North America, and ships from within the continental US.

www.itgovernanceasia.com provides a selected range of ITGP products specifically for customers in

the Indian sub-continent.

www.itgovernance.asia delivers the full range of ITGP publications, serving countries across Asia Pacific. Shipping from Hong Kong, US dollars, Singapore dollars, Hong Kong dollars, New Zealand dollars and Thai baht are all accepted through the website.

Toolkits

ITG's unique range of toolkits includes the IT Governance Framework Toolkit, which contains all the tools and guidance that you will need in order to develop and implement an appropriate IT governance framework for your organisation. For a free paper on how to use the proprietary Calder-Moir IT Governance Framework, and for a free trial version of the toolkit, see *www.itgovernance.co.uk/calder_moir.aspx*.

There is also a wide range of toolkits to simplify implementation of management systems, such as an ISO/IEC 27001 ISMS or an ISO/IEC 22301 BCMS, and these can all be viewed and purchased online at *www.itgovernance.co.uk*.

Training Services

IT Governance offers an extensive portfolio of training courses designed to educate information security, IT governance, risk management and compliance professionals. Our classroom and online training programmes will help you develop the skills required to deliver best practice and compliance to your organisation. They will also enhance your career by providing you with industry-standard certifications and increased peer recognition. Our range of courses offers a structured learning path from foundation to advanced level in the key topics of information security, IT governance, business continuity and service management.

ISO/IEC 20000 is the first international standard for IT service management and has been developed to reflect the best practice guidance contained within the ITIL® framework. Our ISO20000 Foundation and Practitioner training courses are designed to provide delegates with a comprehensive introduction and guide to the implementation of an ISO20000 management system and an industry-recognised qualification awarded by APMG International.

Full details of all IT Governance training courses can be found at *www.itgovernance.co.uk/training.aspx*.

Professional Services and Consultancy

IT service management is becoming increasingly important for organisations. The deployment of best practice frameworks, or the development of a management system that can be certified to ISO/IEC 20000, becomes a greater challenge when the management systems have to be integrated to achieve the most cost-effective and efficient corporate structure.

IT Governance has substantial experience as a professional services company, specialising in IT GRC-related management systems and their integration. Our consulting team can help you design and deploy IT service management structures, such as ITIL and ISO20000, and integrate them with other systems such as, ISO/IEC 27001, ISO22301, ISO14001 and COBIT®. We pride ourselves in being vendor neutral and non-prescriptive in our mentoring approach, whilst transferring the knowledge that you need to document, challenge and improve.

For more information about IT Governance's consultancy services for IT service management see *www.itgovernance.co.uk/itsm-itil-iso20000-consultancy.aspx*.

Publishing Services

IT Governance Publishing (ITGP) is the world's leading IT-GRC publishing imprint that is wholly owned by IT Governance Ltd.

With books and tools covering all IT governance, risk and compliance frameworks, we are the publisher of choice for authors and distributors alike, producing unique and practical publications of the highest quality, in the latest formats available, which readers will find invaluable.

www.itgovernancepublishing.co.uk is the website dedicated to ITGP enabling both current and future authors, distributors, readers and other interested parties, to have easier access to more information. This allows ITGP website visitors to keep up to date with the latest publications and news.

Newsletter

IT governance is one of the hottest topics in business today, not least because it is also the fastest moving.

You can stay up to date with the latest developments across the whole spectrum of IT governance subject matter, including; risk management, information security, ITIL and IT service management, project governance, compliance and so much more, by subscribing to ITG's core publications and topic alert emails.

Simply visit our subscription centre and select your preferences: *www.itgovernance.co.uk/newsletter.aspx*

Trocaire Libraries

CPSIA information can be obtained at www.ICGtesting.com
Printed in the USA
BVOW10s1459270713

327099BV00001B/1/P

9 781849 284561